# Olympic Coast
National Marine Sanctuary

# CONDITION
# REPORT 2008

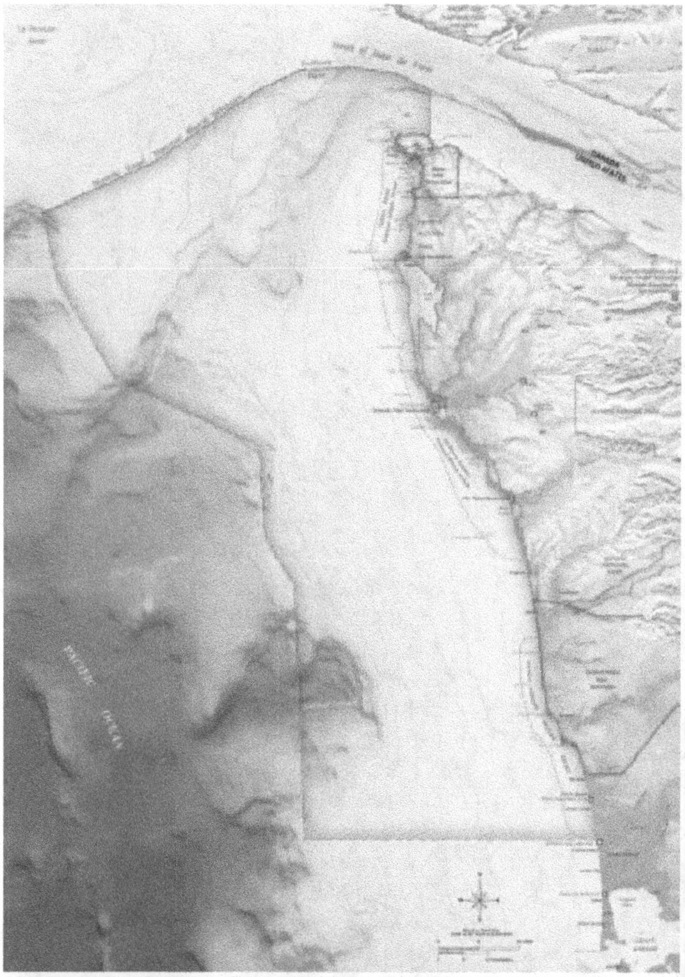

September 2008

NATIONAL MARINE
SANCTUARIES

noaa

U.S. Department of Commerce
Carlos M. Gutierrez, Secretary

National Oceanic and Atmospheric Administration
VADM Conrad C. Lautenbacher, Jr. (USN-ret.)
Under Secretary of Commerce for Oceans and
Atmosphere

National Ocean Service
John H. Dunnigan, Assistant Administrator

Office of National Marine Sanctuaries
Daniel J. Basta, Director

National Oceanic and Atmospheric Administration
Office of National Marine Sanctuaries
SSMC4, N/ORM62
1305 East-West Highway
Silver Spring, MD 20910
301-713-3125
http://sanctuaries.noaa.gov

Olympic Coast National Marine Sanctuary
115 Railroad Ave. East, Suite 301
Port Angeles, WA 98362
(360) 457-6622
http://olympiccoast.noaa.gov

Report Preparation:

Olympic Coast National Marine Sanctuary:
Liam Antrim, John Barimo, Barbara Blackie, Ed Bowlby,
Mary Sue Brancato, George Galasso, Robert Steelquist

Office of National Marine Sanctuaries:
Kathy Broughton, Stephen R. Gittings

Copy Editor: Matt Dozier

Graphic Designer: Matt McIntosh

NATIONAL MARINE
SANCTUARIES

**Cover credits (Clockwise):**

Map:
Bathymetric grids provided by: Divins, D.L. and D. Metzger, NGDC
Coastal Relief Model, Vol. 8, *http://www.ngdc.noaa.gov/mgg/coastal/
coastal.html*

Photos:
Rock Fish: Olympic Coast National Marine Sanctuary; Petro-
glyph: Bob Steelquist, Olympic Coast National Marine Sanctuary;
Elephant Rock: Olympic Coast National Marine Sanctuary; Canoers
during tribal journeys: Bob Steelquist, Olympic Coast National Marine Sanctuary; Kelp Forest: Steve Fisher; Seastars: Nancy Sefton

**Suggested Citation:**
Office of National Marine Sanctuaries. 2008. Olympic Coast National Marine Sanctuary Condition Report 2008. U.S. Department
of Commerce, National Oceanic and Atmospheric Administration,
Office of National Marine Sanctuaries, Silver Spring, MD. 72 pp.

# Table of Contents

## Olympic Coast
## National Marine Sanctuary

- *Designated as a national marine sanctuary in 1994.*

- *The sanctuary extends 217 kilometers (135 miles) along the Washington coast from near Cape Flattery to the Copalis River. Ninety kilometers (56 miles) are shared with Olympic National Park and include some of the last remaining wilderness coastline in the lower 48 states.*

- *The seaward boundary of the sanctuary varies from about 40 to 72 kilometers (25 to 45 miles) offshore. This covers the continental shelf as well as parts of three major submarine canyons. Sanctuary waters include many types of productive marine habitats, including nearshore kelp beds, subtidal reefs, rocky and sandy intertidal zones, submarine canyons, rocky deep-sea habitat, and plankton-rich upwelling zones, all of which support the sanctuary's rich biodiversity.*

- *29 species of marine mammals and over 100 species of seabirds spend at least part of their lives in the sanctuary.*

- *Three national wildlife refuges, collectively called the Washington Island National Wildlife Refuges, are located within the sanctuary. These refuges are part of the Washington Maritime National Wildlife Refuge Complex and protect over 600 named and unnamed offshore rocks, seastacks and islands.*

- *The Olympic Coast has sustained human communities for at least 6,000 years.*

- *The sanctuary lies within the traditional fishing areas for four coastal Indian tribes: the Makah, Quileute and Hoh tribes and the Quinault Indian Nation.*

- *Over 180 documented shipwrecks have historical association with the Olympic Coast.*

## About this Report

This "condition report" provides a summary of resources in the National Oceanic and Atmospheric Administration's Olympic Coast National Marine Sanctuary, pressures on those resources, current condition and trends, and management responses to the pressures that threaten the integrity of the marine environment. Specifically, the document includes information on the status and trends of water quality, habitat, living resources and maritime archaeological resources and the human activities that affect them. It presents responses to a set of questions posed to all sanctuaries (Appendix A). Resource status of Olympic Coast National Marine Sanctuary is rated on a scale from good to poor, and the timelines used for comparison vary from topic to topic. Trends in the status of resources are also reported, and are generally based on observed changes in status over the past five years, unless otherwise specified.

Sanctuary staff consulted with outside experts familiar with the resources and with knowledge of previous and current scientific investigations. Evaluations of status and trends are based on interpretation of quantitative and, when necessary, non-quantitative assessments, and the observations of scientists, managers and users. The ratings reflect the collective interpretation by sanctuary staff of the status of local issues of concern, based on their knowledge and perception of local problems, as rated and informed by outside experts. The final ratings were determined by sanctuary staff. Before public release, this report was peer reviewed to comply with the White House Office of Management and Budget's peer review standards as outlined in the Final Information Quality Bulletin for Peer Review. Further details are provided in Appendix B.

This is the first attempt to describe comprehensively the status, pressures and trends of resources at Olympic Coast National Marine Sanctuary. Additionally, the report helps identify gaps in current monitoring efforts, as well as causal factors that may require monitoring and potential remediation in the years to come. The data discussed will enable resource managers to not only acknowledge prior changes in resource status, but will provide guidance for future management as we face challenges imposed by such potential threats as oil spills, invasive species, commercial development, climate change and underwater noise pollution.

## Summary and Findings

Olympic Coast National Marine Sanctuary represents one of North America's most productive marine ecosystems that lies adjacent to expansive stretches of spectacular undeveloped shoreline. The sanctuary encompasses a variety of habitat types, from sand beaches and rocky intertidal shores to nearshore kelp forests and uninhabited islands, to deep coral and sponge communities and submarine canyons. The sanctuary's temperate location and complex physical environment maintain critical habitats for unique communities of organisms. Twenty-nine species of marine mammals and more than 100 seabird species enrich the system, while fishes occupy a myriad of niches from deep ocean canyons to shallow tide pools. A long history of human interaction with the marine environment is a unique facet of the area's legacy. Native American cultures have lived for millennia in an intimate relationship with the ocean, and beginning in the 16th century, European exploration and settlement made a significant impact on the Olympic Coast.

The overall resources protected by the sanctuary appear to be in good to fair condition. Water quality parameters in the sanctuary appear to be in good condition, which may reflect its isolation from major urban or industrial complexes. There are indications of habitat quality degradation of hard bottom and deep sea biogenic structures that are primarily a result of several decades of bottom contact fishing gear use; however, management decisions have been enacted recently to help reduce this pressure. Living resource conditions have followed trends similar to those of habitats with many seabird, marine mammal and fish population structures significantly altered with respect to historical values. Some uncertainty surrounds our scientific understanding of fishery resources and current levels of exploitation with regards to new initiatives for ecologically based fisheries management that address sustainability of targeted fisheries, as well as marine ecosystem function. Beyond severe natural forces, the principal threats to maritime archaeological resources in the sanctuary come from unauthorized salvage and contact by fishing gear. This condition report will serve as background and supporting material for the review of Olympic Coast National Marine Sanctuary's management plan, which will enable us to better understand, protect and utilize the nation's marine environment.

## National Marine Sanctuary System and System-Wide Monitoring

The National Marine Sanctuary System manages marine areas in both nearshore and open ocean waters that range in size from less than one to almost 362,600 square kilometers (140,000 square miles). Each area has its own concerns and requirements for environmental monitoring, but ecosystem structure and function in all these areas have similarities and are influenced by common factors that interact in comparable ways. Furthermore, the human influences that affect the structure and function of these sites have many similarities. For these reasons, in 2001 the program began to implement System-Wide Monitoring (SWiM). The monitoring framework (National Marine Sanctuary Program 2004) facilitates the development of effective, ecosystem-based monitoring programs that address management information needs using a design process that can be applied in a consistent way at multiple spatial scales and to multiple resource types. It identifies four primary components common among marine ecosystems: water, habitats, living resources and maritime archaeological resources.

By assuming that a common marine ecosystem framework can be applied to all places, the National Marine Sanctuary System developed a series of questions that are posed to every sanctuary and used as evaluation criteria to assess resource conditions and trends. The questions, which are shown on pages vi and vii and explained in Appendix A, are derived from both a generalized ecosystem framework and from the National Marine Sanctuary System's mission. They are widely applicable across the system of areas managed by the Office of National Marine Sanctuaries and provide a tool with which the program can measure its progress toward maintaining and improving natural and archaeological resource quality throughout the system.

Similar reports summarizing resource status and trends will be prepared for each marine sanctuary approximately every five years and updated as new information allows. The information in this report is intended to help set the stage for the management plan review process. The report also helps sanctuary staff identify monitoring, characterization and research priorities to address gaps, day-to-day information needs and new threats.

## Olympic Coast National Marine Sanctuary Condition Summary Table

The following table summarizes the "State of Sanctuary Resources" section of this report. The first two columns list 17 questions used to rate the condition and trends for qualities of water, habitat, living resources, and maritime archaeological resources. The "Rating" column consists of a color, indicating resource condition, and a symbol, indicating trend (see key for definitions). The "Basis for Judgment" column provides a short statement or list of criteria used to justify the rating. The "Description of Findings" column presents the statement that best characterizes resource status, and corresponds to the assigned color rating. The "Description of Findings" statements are customized for all possible ratings for each question. Please see the Appendix for further clarification of the questions and the "Description of Findings" statements.

**Status:** | Good | Good/Fair | Fair | Fair/Poor | Poor | Undet.

**Trends:**
Conditions appear to be improving .................................. ▲
Conditions do not appear to be changing ..................... –
Conditions appear to be declining ............................... ▼
Undetermined trend........................................................ ?
Question not applicable ............................................... N/A

| # | Questions/Resources | Rating | Basis for Judgment | Description of Findings | Sanctuary Response |
|---|---|---|---|---|---|
| **WATER** | | | | | |
| 1 | Are specific or multiple stressors, including changing oceanographic and atmospheric conditions, affecting water quality and how are they changing? | ? | Hypoxic conditions may be increasing in frequency and spatial extent in nearshore waters. | Selected conditions may preclude full development of living resource assemblages and habitats, but are not likely to cause substantial or persistent declines. | Management focuses on oil spill and discharge preventative measures, including relocating ship traffic lanes offshore, tracking ships, enhancing spill response assets in the region, and reducing wastes discharged from ships; moored instruments track nearshore water quality; periodic shipboard surveys are conducted to investigate physical, chemical and biological linkages. |
| 2 | What is the eutrophic condition of sanctuary waters and how is it changing? | – | No suspected human influence on harmful algal blooms or eutrophication. | Conditions do not appear to have the potential to negatively affect living resources or habitat quality. | |
| 3 | Do sanctuary waters pose risks to human health and how are they changing? | – | Naturally occurring harmful algal blooms result in periodic shellfish closures. | Selected conditions that have the potential to affect human health may exist but human impacts have not been reported. | |
| 4 | What are the levels of human activities that may influence water quality and how are they changing? | – | Threat of oil spills from vessels. | Some potentially harmful activities exist, but they do not appear to have had a negative effect on water quality. | |
| **HABITAT** | | | | | |
| 5 | What are the abundance and distribution of major habitat types and how are they changing? | – | Reduction in habitat complexity by bottom-tending gear; short-term impacts from fishing gear and cable installation. | Selected habitat loss or alteration has taken place, precluding full development of living resource assemblages, but it is unlikely to cause substantial or persistent degradation in living resources or water quality. | Sanctuary and partners map and characterize deep habitats and the extent of human impacts and convey information to fisheries managers; large areas have been closed to fishing that uses bottom trawl gear to protect sensitive habitats; negotiated reburial of exposed fiber optic cable; began marine debris removal efforts. |
| 6 | What is the condition of biologically structured habitats and how is it changing? | ? | Damage by bottom-tending gear in some deep biogenic habitats. | Selected habitat loss or alteration may inhibit the development of living resources, and may cause measurable but not severe declines in living resources or water quality. | |
| 7 | What are the contaminant concentrations in sanctuary habitats and how are they changing? | – | Prior studies indicate low levels of contaminants. | Contaminants do not appear to have the potential to negatively affect living resources or water quality. | |
| 8 | What are the levels of human activities that may influence habitat quality and how are they changing? | ▲ | Decrease in bottom trawling and presumably impacts to hard-bottom habitats. | Selected activities have resulted in measurable habitat impacts, but evidence suggests effects are localized, not widespread. | |

**Table is continued on the following page.**

## Olympic Coast National Marine Sanctuary Condition Summary Table (Continued)

| # | Questions/Resources | Rating | Basis for Judgment | Description of Findings | Sanctuary Response |
|---|---|---|---|---|---|
| **LIVING RESOURCES** | | | | | |
| 9 | What is the status of biodiversity and how is it changing? | ? | Ecosystem-level impacts caused by historical depletion of fish, high-order predators, and key-stone species. | Selected biodiversity loss may inhibit full community development and function, and may cause measurable but not severe degradation of ecosystem integrity. | |
| 10 | What is the status of environmentally sustainable fishing and how is it changing? | ▲ | Overexploitation of some groundfish species has led to wide area closures. | Extraction may inhibit full community development and function, and may cause measurable but not severe degradation of ecosystem integrity. | |
| 11 | What is the status of non-indigenous species and how is it changing? | ▼ | Invasive *Sargassum* and tunicate distrubutions are expanding. | Non-indigenous species exist, precluding full community development and function, but are unlikely to cause substantial or persistent degradation of ecosystem integrity. | Sanctuary works with partners to monitor populations of seabirds and marine mammals, to detect non-indigenous species, to conduct regular intertidal monitoring; wide area closures by fisheries management authorities to allow populations to recover. |
| 12 | What is the status of key species and how is it changing? | ? | Populations of Common Murres, sea otters, and numerous rockfish reduced from historic levels, with differing recovery rates. | The reduced abundance of selected keystone species may inhibit full community development and function, and may cause measurable but not severe degradation of ecosystem integrity; or selected key species are at reduced levels, but recovery is possible. | |
| 13 | What is the condition or health of key species and how is it changing? | ? | Diseases detected in sea otters. | The condition of selected key resources is not optimal, perhaps precluding full ecological function, but substantial or persistent declines are not expected. | |
| 14 | What are the levels of human activities that may influence living resource quality and how are they changing? | ▲ | Commercial and recreational fishing pressure has decreased. | Selected activities have resulted in measurable living resource impacts, but evidence suggests effects are localized, not widespread. | |
| **MARITIME ARCHAEOLOGICAL RESOURCES** | | | | | |
| 15 | What is the integrity of known maritime archaeological resources and how is it changing? | ? | Deepwater wrecks stable; shallow wrecks subject to environmental degradation; lack of monitoring to determine trend. | The diminished condition of selected archaeological resources has reduced, to some extent, their historical, scientific, or educational value, and may affect the eligibility of some sites for listing in the National Register of Historic Places. | |
| 16 | Do known maritime archaeological resources pose an environmental hazard and how is this threat changing? | – | Historic wrecks did not carry substantial quantities of hazardous cargoes. | Known maritime archaeological resources pose few or no environmental threats. | Need to conduct inventories and monitoring, and to assess possible impacts of sea level rise on coastal archaeological resources. |
| 17 | What are the levels of human activities that may influence maritime archaeological resource quality and how are they changing? | ? | Fishing activities, cable installations offshore, and unauthorized salvaging. | Selected activities have resulted in measurable impacts to maritime archaeological resources, but evidence suggests effects are localized, not widespread. | |

Figure 1. Olympic Coast National Marine Sanctuary is located off the western shore of Washington state, with a boundary that follows the international border at the north and approximates the 100-fathom (183 m) depth contour. Source: NOAA

# Site History and Resources

Figure 2. Eroded headlands, like this one at Point of Arches, exhibit the continuous dynamic of the sea's forces pounding against the shoreline.

## Overview

Designated in 1994, the sanctuary's mission is to protect the Olympic Coast's natural and cultural resources through responsible stewardship, to conduct and apply research to preserve the area's ecological integrity and maritime heritage, and to promote understanding through public outreach and education.

Olympic Coast National Marine Sanctuary spans 8,572 square kilometers (3,310 square miles) of marine waters off Washington state's rugged Olympic Peninsula coast (Figure 1). Extending seaward 40 to 72 kilometers (25 to 45 miles), the sanctuary covers much of the continental shelf and the heads of three major submarine canyons, in places reaching a maximum depth of over 1,400 meters (4,500 feet). The sanctuary borders an undeveloped coastline, enhancing protection provided by the 90-kilometer-long (56-mile) wilderness of the Olympic National Park's coastal strip, as well as more than 600 offshore islands and emergent rocks within the Washington Islands National Wildlife Refuges (Figure 2). Superimposed on a nutrient-rich upwelling zone with high primary productivity and composed of a multitude of marine habitats, the sanctuary is home to numerous marine mammals and seabirds, diverse populations of kelp and other macroalgae, and diverse fish and invertebrate communities.

## Geology

The Olympic Coast is subject to tectonic forces caused by the combined movements of the large Pacific and North American Plates and the smaller Juan de Fuca Plate. The Juan de Fuca Plate and the Pacific Plate are spreading away from each other at a divergent plate boundary offshore, while the Juan de Fuca plate is being pressed toward and beneath the North American Plate (Figure 3). These forces are linked to a chain of volcanoes within the uplifted Cascade Range. The geologic activity in the area off the Olympic Coast gives rise to potential hazards such as earthquakes and associated submarine landslides, tsunamis and volcanic eruptions. Tsunamis, long-period sea waves produced by submarine earthquakes or volcanoes, occasionally strike the Washington coast. The Alaskan earthquake of 1964 produced a tsunami that reached a height of almost 15 feet (4.5 meters) on the Washington coast south of the sanctuary.

A continental shelf reaches out from Washington's coast from 13 to 64 kilometers (8 to 40 miles), and provides a relatively shallow (200 meters or 660 feet in depth or less) coastal environment within the sanctuary. Several submarine canyons cut into the continental shelf along the western boundary of the sanctuary, and the trough of the Juan de Fuca Canyon winds through the northern portion of the sanctuary towards the Strait of Juan de Fuca. In the northern portion of the sanctuary, the sediments on the shelf are largely glacial deposits from the Ice Age, and the shelf slope is steep and jagged. Modern sediments are carried west through the Strait of Juan de Fuca and north from the Columbia River. These materials are generally transported northward by year-round bottom currents and winter storms, and eventually accumulate on the shelf. The majority of the sanctuary seafloor, however, has not yet been adequately mapped or characterized, so a full understanding of sediments and habitat distribution remains elusive (Intelmann 2006).

Broad beaches, dunes, and ridges dominate the coastline from Cape Disappointment, on the north side of the Columbia River mouth, to the Hoh River. Wave action has eroded the shoreline through time

and has formed steep cliffs at various places along the coast (Figure 2), and forested hills and sloping terraces are found near river mouths. Between Point Grenville and Cape Flattery, cliffs can rise abruptly 15 to 90 meters (50 to 300 feet) above a wave-cut platform that is underwater except during extreme low tides. This wave-cut platform can be almost three kilometers (2 miles) wide in some places. Small islands, sea stacks, and rocks dot the platform's surface.

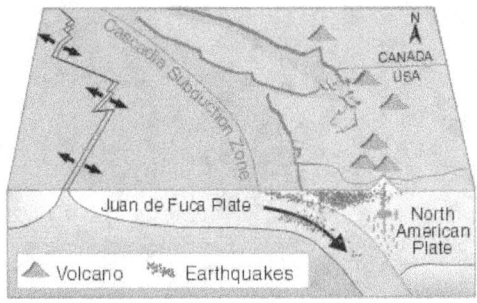

Figure 3. Subduction of the Juan de Fuca Plate under the North American Plate controls the distribution of earthquakes and volcanoes in the Pacific Northwest. Diagram: USGS

Figure 4. Human presence on the Olympic Coast predates historical records and attests to these cultures' long and intricate relationship with the marine environment.

## Original Peoples and European Exploration

The Olympic Coast has sustained human communities for at least 6,000 years and possibly much longer. Native American villages were located at protected harbors and river mouths where people practiced ocean and river-dependent hunting, gathering, fishing and whaling activities (Figure 4). As they are today, Native Americans were among the top or apex predators in the marine ecosystem. Artifacts from one prehistoric site, the Ozette archaeological site near Cape Alava, provide a window into the daily life of that culture immediately before European contact. Clever tools made from natural materials developed from their intimate relationship with natural resources, and complex artwork and rich oral traditions demonstrate the sophistication of these Native American societies. Recent research on earlier sites confirms maritime-adapted cultural practices of offshore fishing and whaling dating at least 4,000 years before present. Today, the Makah, Quileute and Hoh tribes and Quinault Indian Nation carry their heritage forward, balancing the very modern needs of their communities with long traditions. As provided in their treaties with the United States government, treaty tribes share fishery resources with non-tribal residents, and tribes are active as co-managers of the fisheries.

In 1592, Juan de Fuca, a pilot on a Spanish ship, told mariner's tales of visiting a Northwest Passage that emptied into the Pacific Ocean. For the next 200 years, Spain, England, France and Russia all sent explorers to confirm his report and lay claim to the region and its riches. De Fuca's visit was never confirmed, however his name was preserved on later English maps and the passage is now known as the Strait of Juan de Fuca (Figure 1).

In 1778, the English explorer Captain James Cook sailed the coast. In 1788, another English sea captain, John Meares, was so impressed by Mount Olympus that he named it after the mythical home of the Greek gods. "If that be not the home where dwell the Gods, it is beautiful enough to be, and I therefore call it Mount Olympus," he wrote. The name was made official 14 years later when Captain George Vancouver entered the name on his maps and referred to the whole range as the Olympic Mountains. Although the Spanish built the first European settlement near Neah Bay in 1792, Spanish influence was short-lived. The settlement was abandoned after only five months when Spain came under the threat of war from Great Britain.

## Commerce

Furs were the key to opening the northwest coast to European trade in the late 1700s, especially profitable sea otter pelts that were obtained from the Indians by English, Russian, Spanish and American fur traders. As the news spread of the great profits to be had in fur trading, sea otter populations dwindled and by the early 1900s, sea otters had been extirpated from Washington waters (Figure 5).

Photo: Ed Bowlby, Olympic Coast National Marine Sanctuary

Figure 5. Sea otters in the Northeast Pacific were hunted nearly to extinction in the 18th and 19th centuries for their fur. Because of reintroduction efforts in the 1970s to the Pacific Northwest, they are making a comeback along the Olympic coast.

## Coastal Tribes of the outer coast of Washington - (from south to north)

| | |
|---|---|
| *Quinault Indian Nation* | *The Quinault Indian Nation consists of the Quinault and Queets tribes and descendants of five other coastal tribes. The Quinault Indian Reservation, located in the southwest corner of the Olympic Peninsula, includes 37 kilometers (23 miles) of Pacific coastline and covers 84,271 hectares (208,150 acres) of forested land.* |
| *Hoh Indian Tribe* | *The Hoh Reservation consists of 179 hectares (443 acres) located 45 kilometers (28 miles) south of Forks at the mouth of the Hoh River. The reservation has about 1.6 kilometers (1 mile) of beachfront between the mouth of the Hoh River and Ruby Beach.* |
| *Quileute Indian Tribe* | *Surrounded on three sides by the Olympic National Park, the Quileute Reservation is located on 451 hectares (1,115 acres) along the Pacific Ocean on the south banks of the Quillayute River and includes the town of LaPush.* |
| *Makah Indian Tribe* | *Located in the northwestern most corner of the contiguous U.S., the Makah Reservation consists of 11,007 hectares (27,200 acres) and is bounded by the Pacific Ocean and the Strait of Juan de Fuca. It includes the town of Neah Bay. Over 405 hectares (1,000 acres) of the land bordering the Pacific Ocean have been reserved as a wilderness area. The Makah are part of the Nootkan culture group, which includes two other tribes in British Columbia, Canada.* |

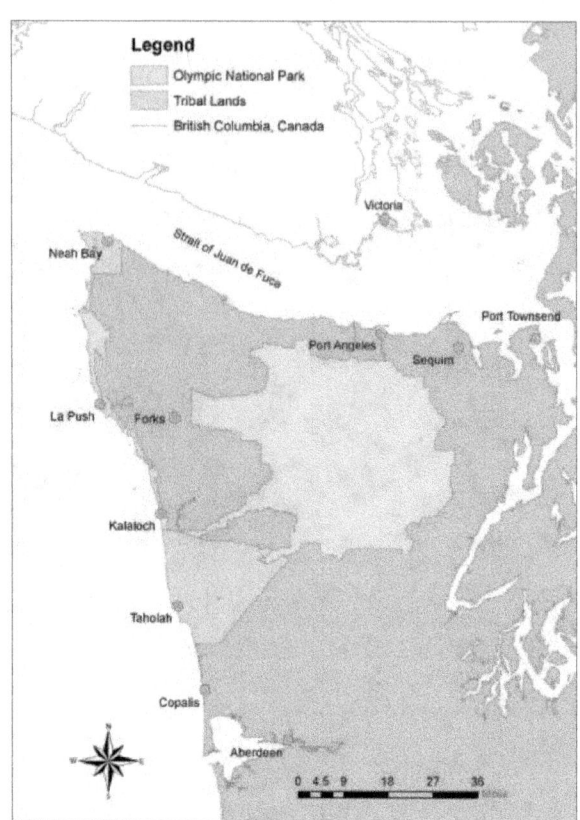

Figure 6. Most current-day cities and towns around the Olympic Peninsula grew from Native American village sites. Diagram: OCNMS

Figure 7. Southward-blowing winds are associated with a net transport of surface waters away from the coastline, resulting in intermittent upwelling. Image: Oregon Sea Grant

Through the latter part of the 1800s, pioneers moved into the Olympic Peninsula to farm, fish, and cut timber. Like Native Americans, most early settlers chose to settle along the coast. In 1851, Port Townsend became the first permanent American settlement on the peninsula, providing a gateway for further settlements to the west (Figure 6). Port Angeles, with its harbor, lighthouse, military reservation, customs house, and strategic location on the Strait of Juan de Fuca, was designated by President Abraham Lincoln as a town site in 1862. Today, it is the peninsula's largest town, with a population of 18,400 (in 2000). Farther west, the town of Forks had European settlers as early as the 1860s. People were originally drawn to Forks for gold prospects, but timber became the mainstay of the economy of Forks and other west end towns. Fishing continues to be an important commercial and recreational venture for coastal communities like Neah Bay and La Push.

Although the area attracted logging, farming and fishing interests, the rugged western coast and interior of the peninsula retain significant roadless wilderness. Olympic National Park was established in 1938 and now includes nearly a million acres of mountain, forest, and coastline designated as wilderness. The coastal strip of the park was added in 1953. The Olympic National Forest was designated in 1897 as the Olympic Forest Reserve and now contains 88,265 acres (15 percent of the total national forest acreage) of designated wilderness.

Throughout the period of European settlement on the western Olympic Peninsula, the link between the land and the ocean has shaped history. All coastal trade vessels working between California and Puget Sound, as well as vessels visiting the region for trans-Pacific trade, traversed the area that is now the sanctuary. The lumber trade on the Pacific Coast was a long-lived and very significant aspect of maritime trade along the coast. Beginning in the 1850s with the establishment of sawmills on Puget Sound and environs, larger vessels, many of them veterans of the California Gold Rush, commenced the trade. Early canneries, logging operations and hotels reflected not just the economic opportunities offered by coastal resources, but the hardships imposed by the Olympic Coast's remoteness, such as lack of or limited road transport. Coast-wide trade linked the productive Olympic Peninsula with Seattle and markets in California, Hawaii, Australia and beyond. In addition, the completion of railroad links across the Continental Divide in both Canada and the United States made the ports of Vancouver, Seattle, Everett, Tacoma and Victoria important sources of grain, timber, gold and other resources for the world's economy.

Today, commerce on the Olympic coast still depends largely on commercial and recreational fishing, logging and tourism. In recent years, the local timber industry and the fishing industries have both been impacted by reduced harvests, and the local economy has struggled.

Coastal communities continue to respond to a changing economy by developing innovative enterprises such as value-added wood product manufacturing (local manufacturing rather than export of raw timber) and accommodating the growth of tourism to diversify the economic base.

## Water

The Washington outer coast is known for its rough seas and large waves — extreme wave heights ranging from 15 to 27 meters (50 to 90 feet) have been recorded on and beyond the continental shelf. Winter storms travel across the fetch of the Pacific and the energy is magnified as they encounter the shallower continental shelf, where their force pounds the coast with gathered intensity.

Surface winds generated by atmospheric pressure systems are the main force driving ocean surface circulation off the Pacific Northwest. Spring and summer winds blow generally toward the south and push surface waters southward and offshore. This results in nearshore upwelling of cold, nutrient-rich water to the surface (Figure 7). This influx of nutrients enhances plankton communities that are ultimately responsible for the region's productive fisheries. Downwelling tends to occur in the fall and winter months, when the winds blow generally toward the north and surface water is forced shoreward. Other physical features also play a role in these movements: Shelf platform width, river plumes, submarine canyons, banks, coastal promontories and offshore eddies influence the retention, magnitude and timing of nutrient delivery to plankton, and may explain why primary productivity is higher along the Washington coast than the Oregon coast (Hickey and Banas 2003).

On a regional scale, the California Current transports cold subarctic water southward along the Washington coast, directly influencing the local distribution of marine organisms. The California Current generally occurs from the continental shelf break to a distance of about 1,000 kilometers from shore and rides above the narrower California Undercurrent, which flows northward and is implicated in the transport of larvae and other plankton. The California Current and Undercurrent are strongest in the summer, while the seasonal, nearshore Davidson current flows northward during winter months when the Columbia River plume is transported along the Washington coast. Another seasonal feature is the Juan de Fuca Eddy, which is approximately 50 kilometers in diameter, persists in summertime, and entrains nutrient-rich cold water in a counterclockwise circulation pattern (see Figure 19, page 23).

Oceanographic and atmospheric events across the Pacific basin influence the waters of the Olympic Coast. For example, the El Niño-

Figure 8. Within the nearshore environment, kelp forests are vital habitat for many species of fish, invertebrates, seabirds and mammals.

Southern Oscillation is primarily driven by sea surface temperatures along the Equatorial Pacific Ocean and is a major source of inter-annual climate variability in the Pacific Northwest, with events lasting 6 to 18 months. Similarly, the Pacific Decadal Oscillation is a predominant source of climate variability in the Pacific Northwest, where warm or cool phases can each last 20 to 30 years. Climatic cycles such as these are natural events and often are associated with strong fluctuations in weather patterns and biological resources.

## Habitat

Olympic Coast National Marine Sanctuary contains a broad diversity of habitats including rocky shores, sandy beaches, kelp forests, sea stacks and islands, open ocean or pelagic habitats, the continental shelf seafloor and submarine canyons. Along the shoreline, tide pools are formed amid boulders and rocky outcrops that provide both temporary and permanent homes for an abundance of "seaweeds" (e.g., macroalgae and seagrasses), invertebrate species such as sea stars, hermit crabs, and sea anemones, and intertidal fish. Rocky shores of the Olympic Coast have among the highest biodiversity of marine invertebrates and macroalgae of all eastern Pacific coastal sites from Central America to Alaska (Suchanek 1979; PISCO 2002; Blanchette et al. in press). Nestled between these rocky headlands are numerous sand-covered pocket beaches that host their unique array of intertidal invertebrates and fishes.

Kelp forests form dense stands in nearshore waters, with individual plants reaching up to 20 meters in length (Figure 8). The structure of this living habitat alters the physical forces (waves and currents) in the nearshore area and creates a protective environment for fish

Figure 9. The red tree coral with darkblotched and sharpchin rockfish are colorful inhabitants of deep rocky areas.

Figure 10. Most killer whales (or orca) in the sanctuary belong to resident groups that frequent northern Puget Sound and the Strait of Georgia. Occasionally, wide-ranging oceanic groups (transient orca and offshore orca) visit the region.

and invertebrates, from their holdfast bases on the seafloor to their canopies at the surface. Sea otters often raft and rest in and near kelp canopies, while many species and ages of fish find protective habitat among the kelp forests.

Pinnacles (sea stacks) and islands along the coast also provide havens and resting sites for California and Steller sea lions, harbor and elephant seals, and thousands of nesting seabirds. High-relief submerged topographic features such as rock piles serve as fish aggregation areas.

A majority of the sanctuary lies over the continental shelf, extending from the nearshore to the shelf break at about the 200-meter contour. The shelf is composed primarily of soft sediment and glacial deposits of cobble, gravel and boulders, punctuated by rock outcrops, and it is inhabited by creatures such as flatfish, rockfish, octopuses, brittle stars and sea pens that have adapted to the darkness, cold, and pressure of the seafloor. Sanctuary boundaries extend beyond the edge of the continental shelf and include portions of the Nitinat, Juan de Fuca, and Quinault submarine canyons (Figure 1). The Quinault canyon is the deepest, descending to 1,420 meters (4,660 feet) at its deepest point within the sanctuary. Many creatures, such as corals, sponges, crinoids, rockfish and shrimp, inhabit these areas of physical extremes. The canyons are also dynamic areas where massive submarine landslides can occur on the steep side walls, undetected by man, and canyon bottoms collect sediment deposited from above. They also serve as conduits for dense, cold, nutrient-rich seawater that is pulled toward shore, where upwelling feeds surface productivity at the base of the food web.

Recent surveys conducted in offshore shelf and canyon habitats have confirmed the presence of hard-bottom substrates that harbor rich invertebrate assemblages, including deepwater coral and sponges (Brancato et al. 2007). Such fauna are commonly thought to be restricted to shal-

low tropical waters. However, an increasing number of studies around the world have recorded coral and sponge assemblages in deeper, cold-water habitats at both northern and southern latitudes. These living organisms with branching, upright structure are, in turn, habitat for other invertebrates and fish (Whitmire and Clarke 2007). Habitat-forming corals and sponges provide hiding places, attachment sites, food sources, and breeding and nursery grounds in relatively inhospitable and otherwise featureless environments (Figure 9).

## Living Resources

Twenty-nine species of marine mammals have been sighted in Olympic Coast National Marine Sanctuary, including eight species listed under the Endangered Species Act. Two species are frequent foragers in the sanctuary: the humpback whale and the killer whale (also called orca) (Figure 10). Gray whales, which were recently removed from the endangered species list, travel through the sanctuary on their annual migrations between breeding and calving grounds off the Baja Peninsula and summer feeding grounds in the northern Pacific. Sea otters, harbor and elephant seals, and Steller and California sea lions aggregate along the shore and haul out on land at many locations along the coast throughout the year.

Seabirds are the most conspicuous members of the offshore fauna of the Olympic Coast. Sea stacks and islands provide critical nesting habitat for 19 species of marine birds and marine-associated raptors and shorebirds, including seven alcid species (murres, puffins, murrelets, etc., Figure 11), three cormorant species, four gull and tern species, two stormpetrel species, two raptors and one shorebird, the Black Oystercatcher. Productive offshore waters attract large feeding aggregations of marine birds that breed in other regions of the world but travel great distances to "winter" in sanctuary waters. The Sooty Shearwater, for example, breeds

Figure 11. The distinctive Tufted Puffin is a familiar seabird that nests in burrows on remote islands far from any mammalian predators.

Figure 12. Nearly every surface in the rocky intertidal zone is used by something, and space is at a premium. Predatory ochre sea stars search for mussels among communities of green sea anemones and rockweed.

along the coasts of New Zealand and Chile in the austral summer and congregates along the Pacific coast in its non-breeding season. Black-footed and Laysan Albatross travel far from their breeding grounds in Hawaii and Japan to forage in the eastern Pacific. Nearer to shore, sand and gravel beaches furnish foraging areas for shorebirds, crows, gulls and a host of other birds and mammals. The coastline forms an important migratory pathway for millions of birds that pass through each year, guiding waterfowl, cranes, shorebirds and raptors toward northern breeding areas during the spring and southward as winter approaches.

Sanctuary waters are inhabited by diverse and abundant fish and invertebrate populations (Figure 12). Commercially important fish and shellfish include at least 30 species of rockfish (including 13 state species of concern, of which three are also federal species of concern), plus Pacific halibut, herring, Pacific cod, Pacific whiting, lingcod, sablefish, 15 or more species of flatfish, Dungeness crab, razor clams, and several species of shrimp. Five species of Pacific salmon (chinook, sockeye, pink, chum and coho) occur along the outer coast of Washington and breed in the Olympic Peninsula's rivers and streams. Three similar salmonid species found in freshwater systems (sea-run cutthroat trout, bull trout, and steelhead) spend portions of their lives in nearshore marine waters. Olympic Coast populations of Ozette sockeye and bull trout were added to the federal list of threatened species in 1999. Nearshore habitats of the sanctuary are important for salmon that spawn in adjacent streams. The sanctuary also encompasses the migration corridor of both juvenile and adult salmonids from California, Oregon and British Columbia, and from other rivers in Washington. Sharks, albacore, sardines, mackerel, anchovies and other migratory species are also found in the sanctuary seasonally. These fast-moving fishes are important resources for tribal and non-tribal fishers.

Intertidal habitats challenge inhabitants with extreme temperature,

salinity and oxygen fluctuations, along with powerful physical forces such as sand scouring and wave action. Invertebrate communities in rocky intertidal zones are some of the richest on the West Coast and include a wide diversity of sea stars, sea urchins, nudibranchs, chitons and polychaetes. Macroalgae or seaweeds are also extremely diverse in the region, with an estimated 120 species thought to occur within the sanctuary rocky intertidal zone (Dethier 1988). Sandy intertidal areas host sand-dwelling invertebrates and several notable fish species including starry flounder, staghorn sculpin, sand lance, sand sole, surfperch and sanddab. Surf smelt spawn at high tide on sand-gravel beaches where surf action bathes and aerates the eggs. Rocky intertidal habitats hold another roster of residents: tidepool sculpins, gunnels, eelpouts, pricklebacks, cockcombs and warbonnets, to name few.

In the deeper areas of the sanctuary (greater than 80 meters or 250 feet) investigations have revealed stunning colonies of brightly colored, cold-water corals and sponges. These unique assemblages include soft corals such as gorgonian species, stony corals (e.g., *Lophelia* spp.), giant cup corals (e.g., *Desmophyllum* spp.) and at least 40 species of sponges (Brancato et al. 2007). The distribution of such deepwater communities, as well as their species richness and basic biology, are unknown but are currently under scientific investigation.

## Maritime Archaeological Resources
### *Native and Prehistoric Maritime Heritage*

The modern shoreline of the Olympic Peninsula contains dozens of late prehistoric archaeological sites that are rich in materials documenting the character of the maritime environment and the use of this environment by the region's native peoples. Nearshore coastal forests adjacent to the sanctuary contain mid-Holocene shorelines and older prehistoric archaeological sites. These older sites are rich

Figure 13. Surveyed shipwrecks in Olympic Coast National Marine Sanctuary. Source: OCNMS

in materials documenting the character of maritime paleo-environments, the history of environmental change, and the record of use of these environments by the region's native peoples.

The earliest dated archaeological site on the Washington Coast occurs adjacent to the sanctuary on the Makah Indian Reservation, establishing human presence for the last 6,000 years. Although complex geological and climatic factors have changed the shoreline due to tectonic uplift and global sea level rise, it is evident that humans have occupied the coastal zone and adapted to changing habitats over time. The recent investigation of paleoshoreline sites on the

Makah Reservation reveals high sea-stand village sites inland along the Sooes and Waatch river valleys, in some cases greater than 10 meters above current sea level and kilometers from the current ocean shore (Wessen 2003). These sites indicate complex interactions with marine resources of the period and yield important clues to large-scale ocean and climate regimes, marine wildlife and fish populations, habitat distribution and cultural patterns of marine resource use. Late prehistoric cultural patterns are particularly well documented. The Makah Cultural and Research Center in Neah Bay houses an extraordinary collection of artifacts from the Ozette archaeological site, a Makah village that was partially buried by a mudslide nearly 500 years ago and excavated in the 1970s. Items used for research and display include whaling, seal hunting and fishing gear.

Other tangible records of prehistoric human occupation include petroglyphs — both above the intertidal zone and within it — and canoe runs, or channels cleared of boulders to facilitate landing of dugout watercraft. Research and preservation of coastal native languages, traditional cultural properties, and traditional practices of song, dance and activities like whaling also enhances awareness in native and non-native peoples of the region's rich ocean-dependent heritage. The recent resurgence of the canoe culture in the annual "Tribal Journeys" celebration transfers knowledge and understanding of coastal culture to new generations.

### Historic Maritime Heritage

Olympic Coast National Marine Sanctuary is one of the more significant and unique maritime cultural landscapes in the United States. It lies at the entrance to a major inland maritime highway, the Inside Passage to Alaska, as well as serving as the gateway to several historically significant and active ports. The combination of fierce weather, isolated and rocky shores, and thriving ship commerce have, on many occasions, made the Olympic Coast a graveyard for ships. More than 180 shipwrecks have been documented in the vicinity of the Olympic Coast through a literature review, yet only a few have been investigated using modern survey techniques (Figure 13). There are few recorded shipwrecks prior to the mid-19th century and no verified wrecks during the 18th century. The number of vessel losses increased significantly as Puget Sound developed into an economic center and as Victoria, British Columbia, developed on the north side of the Strait of Juan de Fuca in the 19th century. The 19th-century lumber trade, in particular, greatly expanded vessel traffic — for example, more than 600

Photo Olympic Coast National Marine Sanctuary

Figure 14. The wild coastline leading to the western entrance of the Strait of Juan de Fuca, the passageway for ships bound to major ports in the Pacific Northwest, is unforgiving to vessels whose bearings, visibility or propulsion are compromised.

vessels entered and cleared Puget Sound past Cape Flattery in 1886. Ship losses were predominantly weather-related and included founderings, collisions and groundings. Many ships simply disappeared, their last known location recorded by the lighthouse keeper at Tatoosh Island before they disappeared into watery oblivion (Figure 14).

Historic structures on land, while technically outside of sanctuary boundaries, remain as important tangible fragments of the past and provide insight into past human interactions with the ocean. These include historic lighthouses at Tatoosh and Destruction islands, lifesaving station remnants at Waadah Island and LaPush, wartime defense sites at Cape Flattery and Anderson Point, and sites of coastal patrol cabins scattered along the Olympic Coast. Homesteads, resorts, graves, and memorials also reflect a human dimension to the coast now largely reclaimed by time, the forest, or the sea.

# Pressures on the Sanctuary

Human activities and natural processes both affect the condition of natural and archaeological resources in marine sanctuaries. This section describes the nature and extent of the most prominent human influences upon Olympic Coast National Marine Sanctuary.

## Commercial Development

With advances in technologies and changes in our society's needs come proposals for new projects, many of which could not have been anticipated at the time of the sanctuary's designation and are not addressed in the existing management plan. The design of these developments and their potential impacts must be carefully considered to assess their compatibility with the sanctuary's primary goal of resource protection.

### Fiber Optic Telecommunications

In 1999-2000, a pair of trans-Pacific fiber optic telecommunication cables, called the Pacific Crossing-1 (PC-1) system, was laid across the northern portion of the sanctuary en route from Mukilteo, Washington, to Japan. Submarine cable installation involves substantial seafloor disturbance along a narrow swath as a plow cuts about a meter into the substrate to bury and protect the cable and to avoid future entanglement with anchors, fishing gear or organisms. Although successful cable burial was reported, surveys of the PC-1 cables in the sanctuary conducted in 2000 revealed that substantial portions of each cable were not buried at a sufficient depth to avoid risks, and in many places the cables were unburied and suspended above the seafloor. In this condition, the cables could be physically damaged by fishing trawl gear and require repairs that could repeatedly disturb seafloor communities. Additionally, where unburied and suspended, the cables pose a serious safety concern for fishers employed in bottom contact fisheries who could snag gear on an exposed cable, a risk that limits access of Native American tribal fishers to portions of their treaty-reserved fishing grounds. In light of these risks, the cable owners agreed to recover and re-lay the cables in the sanctuary, an effort that was completed in late summer 2006 (NOAA 2005, Tyco 2006).

### Proposed Ocean Wave Energy Project

The Makah Bay Offshore Wave Energy Pilot Project has been in development for several years and is currently undergoing environmental review and permitting approvals. In December 2007, this project was issued a conditional license by the Federal Energy Regulatory Commission; this is the first federal license for an ocean energy project in the U.S. This one-megawatt demonstration project would test a novel technology and deliver power to the Clallam County Public Utility District's grid from a renewable, "green" energy source — ocean waves. As proposed, the project includes four interconnected, floating buoys tethered to the ocean floor with a complex anchoring system and a submarine electrical transmission cable laid across the seabed to the shore and routed underground past sensitive nearshore habitat. Authorization from the sanctuary will be required, but the project proponent has not yet applied for a sanctuary permit.

The in-water portion of the project is within Olympic Coast sanctuary boundaries, and the shore-based facilities are on tribal land of the Makah Indian Nation. The development company, Finavera Renewables, has conducted preliminary site evaluation studies and is developing final designs and plans for the installations. Federal, state and tribal representatives are working with Finavera to develop maintenance and monitoring plans to mitigate and assess potential environmental impacts of this new technology, including damage to seafloor habitats and threats to marine mammals and seabirds (FERC 2007).

### Open-Ocean Aquaculture

NOAA's Aquaculture Program is currently exploring possibilities for open-ocean or offshore aquaculture production in federal waters, which include all sanctuary waters more than three nautical miles (5.5 kilometers) off the Washington coast. Open-ocean aquaculture is a controversial issue for some segments of the public and raises regulatory concerns with regard to pathogens, nutrient loading, fishing area restrictions and habitat and ecosystem impacts. To date, no projects have been proposed for open-ocean aquaculture in the sanctuary. Although sea conditions are dynamic and challenging in the sanctuary, technological developments in anchoring and structural design may make such development feasible in the sanctuary in the future. If projects are proposed for the sanctuary, it will be necessary for sanctuary staff to investigate potential environmental impacts and weigh these against sanctuary goals and mandates while making permitting decisions.

## Fishing

Commercial and recreational fishing are important components of the coastal economy and provide valuable food resources to the Northwest and beyond. Fishing occurs within the sanctuary, and commercial, tribal and recreational fishers are significant stakeholders in the health of the fisheries. However, some aspects of fishing practices and regulations are under scrutiny from co-managers for their potential negative impacts to habitat and to ecosystem functions.

In recent years, the NOAA Fisheries Service has implemented regulations on the West Coast to restore stocks of overfished species and prevent physical damage to Essential Fish Habitat. Research has documented damage to deep coral and sponge communities by bottom contact fishing gear around the world (Fosså et al. 2002, Morgan et

2005, Rogers 2004, Morgan et al. 2006). The distribution of existing and historic deep coral and sponge communities in the Olympic Coast region is poorly known, as is the extent of impact to those areas (Brancato et al. 2007).

Rough waters and complex seabed features of the sanctuary increase the potential for fishing gear entanglement and loss. Studies from Puget Sound and beyond reveal that abandoned fishing gear can remain for decades, potentially entangling and killing species that encounter the gear (NRC Inc. 2008). This phenomenon has been called "ghost fishing," where derelict gear continues to fish by attract-

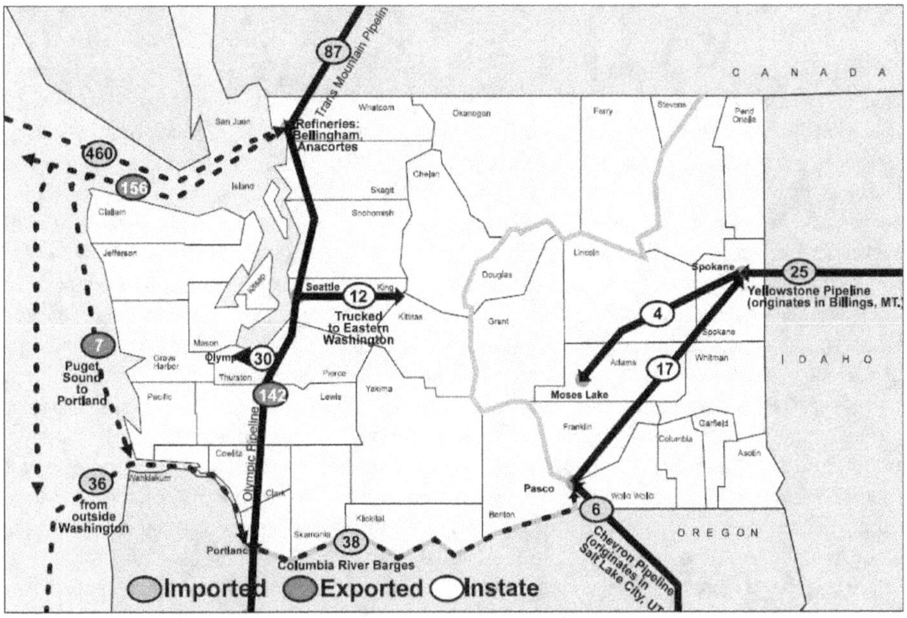

Figure 15. Primary transportation routes and quantities of petroleum products transported in Washington state, with specific routes scaled in thousands of barrels per day. Source: Washington State Department of Ecology

ing, trapping and killing a wide variety of marine mammals, seabirds, shellfish and other invertebrates, and fish. Dead organisms attract other feeding animals, thus perpetuating the cycle of unintended mortality. A direct economic impact of ghost fishing is the reduction of fishery stocks otherwise available for commercial and recreational fishers. Accumulations of gear on critical spawning and rearing habitat can significantly impact fishery stocks. Derelict fishing gear also can threaten human safety, restrict other legitimate sanctuary uses — such as regulated fishing, anchoring and operation of vessels — and diminish the aesthetic qualities for activities such as scuba diving.

## Ballast Water and Invasive Species

Millions of liters of seawater are routinely carried around the world as ballast aboard oil tankers and other commercial vessels to increase stability. If ships empty their ballast tanks of water transported from other regions there is a risk of introducing non-native fish, invertebrates and plants, many of which can alter ecosystems, sometimes in catastrophic ways. Washington state recently implemented regulations to minimize this risk by requiring ballast water treatment or exchange in offshore waters beyond the sanctuary. Still, invasive species can also be introduced through hull fouling, smaller commercial and recreational vessels, aquaculture practices, release of captive animals and plants (e.g., aquarium specimens), floating marine debris, or range expansion.

Several established and emerging non-indigenous invaders, such as the invasive alga *Sargassum muticum* and the European green crab, *Carcinus maenas*, threaten both critical habitat and important commercial species in the Pacific Northwest. There is widespread recognition that invasive species can affect fisheries, waterways and facilities operating adjacent to waterways, as well as the functioning of natural ecosystems. The introduction of aquatic invasive species into the coastal waters of the Pacific Northwest poses serious economic and environmental threats recognized by resource managers, the aquaculture industry, non-governmental organizations and concerned citizens. Coastal estuaries in Washington, which provide critical habitat for many commercially important species such as Dungeness crab, shellfish and many marine fish species, are particularly susceptible to rapid development of aquatic invasive species populations.

## Oil Spills

As one of North America's major gateways to Pacific Rim trade, the Strait of Juan de Fuca is one of the busiest waterways in the world, with vessel traffic going to several busy ports in Washington state and Vancouver, British Columbia. Every year, approximately 5,000 vessels greater than 300 gross tons transit the northern part of the sanctuary on approach to the Strait of Juan de Fuca, and a comparable number of outbound transits occur immediately north of the sanctuary in Canadian waters.

Washington is also one of the nation's primary petroleum refining centers. Tank vessels inbound to Puget Sound move crude oil to Washington's refineries. Large quantities of crude oil also come into refineries through the Trans Mountain Pipeline from Canada. Refined products are exported from Washington to other western states primarily through pipelines, barges and tankers. These transportation corridors are at greatest risk to major spills (Figure 15) (WDOE 2007) http://www.ecy.wa.gov/pubs/97252.pdf. Cargo, fishing and passenger vessels involved with Pacific Rim commerce can also hold substantial quantities of petroleum products in their fuel tanks.

Oil contamination of marine mammals and seabirds can cause eye irritation, impairment of thermal regulation, loss of buoyancy, toxicity, reproductive abnormalities, and ultimately death. Oil spills can deplete food sources and destroy habitat characteristics essential for survival of vertebrate species. A spill could wipe out at least one generation of a population, and in a worst-case scenario, extinguish multiple species on a local or regional scale. Sea otters and many species of seabirds that inhabit or utilize the ocean's surface are particularly susceptible to damage from oil in nearshore environments.

Oil spills can have lethal as well as long-term, sub-lethal effects on fish (e.g., behavioral changes, reproductive abnormalities) and can also contaminate fish targeted for human consumption. Some sectors of the fishing and shellfish industries could be shut down for years by an oil spill, causing long-term negative effects on the economy of local tribes and other coastal fishers. Nearshore habitats, critical for survival of juvenile fish, can also be severely impacted by oil spills that smother or poison kelp, sea grasses and other marine plants. Oiling of intertidal areas can cause significant damage to invertebrates, with negative impacts that can linger for many years (Downs et al. 2002).

The Washington coast has endured the damages of several oil spills in recent times, including the 1988 Nestucca barge spill, which released 231,000 gallons of fuel oil into waters off Grays Harbor, impacting many kilometers of coastline as far north as Canada. In 1991, a fishing vessel, Tenyo Maru, spilled 100,000 gallons of diesel fuel that spread as far south as Oregon but most heavily impacted the Makah Indian Reservation and Olympic National Park wilderness coast. Although state and federal oil spill prevention and response policies are continually improving, the potential for severe environmental damage remains a strong concern in the region.

## Increased Human Use

Long-time residents as well as day-use visitors are drawn to the many recreational opportunities of the Olympic Coast, including sport fishing, kayaking, surfing, wildlife viewing, clamming and beachcombing. Recreational use can sometimes cause unintended pressures to the coastal ecosystem. Motorized and non-motorized recreational boaters and sight-seeing pilots can inadvertently disturb wildlife, often with

devastating consequences. Although human access to most seabird colonies is restricted by the U.S. Fish and Wildlife Service's WA Maritime Refuge Complex regulations (USFWS 2007), wildlife on the refuge islands is vulnerable to disturbance from low-flying aircraft that do not comply with the 2,000-foot elevation requirement established by the sanctuary. Cliff-nesting seabirds can abandon their nests if frightened, leaving eggs and nestlings exposed to avian predators. Resting pinnipeds can abandon their haulout sites for the water when disturbed, often at a large energetic cost, especially to young animals. Beach users such as bird watchers, dog walkers, ATV users and surfers can displace foraging migratory birds at important resting and staging areas. Popular intertidal areas show signs of trampling in localized patches.

Watershed alterations from increased land use such as timber harvesting may affect water quality by increasing sediment loads and nutrient runoff. Excessive sediment introduced to the nearshore environment can suffocate benthic marine life and reduce water clarity. Some persistent industrial chemicals, even those no longer in use in this country such as DDT, have found their way into marine food webs and can be detected in tissue samples of higher-order predators (Brancato et al. 2006, Ross et al. 2000, Ross 2006). Some are carried from land to sea through watersheds, while others may be transported via air currents.

Garbage and lost fishing gear — particularly items composed of non-biodegradable products like plastic — are elements of what is collectively called marine debris. The amount of marine debris in open-ocean and coastal systems is on the rise throughout the world. Impacts from marine debris include entanglement and drowning of animals, inadvertent ingestion of plastics by mammals, turtles and birds, transfer of diseases from land-based sources to marine wildlife, fouling of active fishing gear, and benthic habitat degradation.

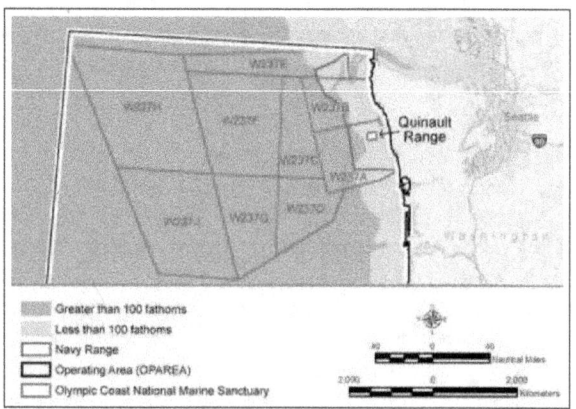

Figure 16. Operations areas for the U.S. Navy off the northern Washington coast. The green line is the boundary of Olympic Coast National Marine Sanctuary. Source: adapted from U.S. Navy

## Military Activities

In or adjacent to the sanctuary, the military has pre-established training areas that are part of the Northwest Training Range Complex. These training areas include two warning areas (W-237A and W-237B) and two military operation areas (MOA Olympic A and B) that are designated training and operating areas for the Pacific Fleet air and surface forces (Figure 16). Military activities in these areas consist of subsurface, offshore surface, aerial training activities, and other military operations as discussed in the sanctuary's original environmental impact statement (NOAA 1993). Military operations that are exempt from sanctuary regulations include:

■ Hull integrity tests and other deepwater tests

■ Live firing of guns, missiles, torpedoes and chaff

■ Activities associated with the Quinault Range including the in-water testing of non-explosive torpedoes; and

■ Anti-submarine warfare operations

The Navy's Underwater Warfare Center (NUWC) Division Keyport operates and maintains the Quinault Underwater Tracking Range located in Navy Operations Area W-237A. This range is instrumented to track surface vessels, submarines and various undersea vehicles. It is the policy of NUWC Division Keyport not to test in the presence of cetaceans. The Navy has proposed expansion of the Quinault Range's area more than 50-fold to support existing and future needs in manned and unmanned vehicle programs development. The proposed geographic expansion would include a surf-zone landing site.

Potential effects associated with Navy research, development, testing and evaluation, and fleet training activities are currently being evaluated in separate environmental impact statements (EIS) via the National Environmental Policy Act (NEPA) process. The Navy has proposed extending the Quinault Range site activities and geographic boundaries to support existing and future needs in manned and unmanned vehicle programs development. The extension would coincide with the existing W-237A Military Warning Area and one surf-zone access site. The Navy has no plan under this EIS to extend any permanent bottom-mounted instrumentation by the proposed action, but has proposed temporary installations on the seafloor. The fleet training activities are being evaluated under a separate, ongoing NEPA process. During scoping, the Olympic Coast Sanctuary Advisory Council requested that this review consider a wide variety of issues, including: disturbance to birds, fish, and mammals from increased activity and noise; damage to seafloor habitats and wildlife from cables, anchors, targets, torpedoes and unmanned undersea vehicles; accidental discharges of pollutants; interference with tribal fishing and subsistence harvest activities; and restrictions on the ability of sanctuary and affiliated scientists to conduct research.

## Underwater Noise Pollution

The level of noise pollution in the oceans has increased dramatically during the last 50 years. The primary source of low-frequency ocean noise is commercial shipping (NRC 2003). Although impacts to wildlife in the Olympic Coast sanctuary have not been documented, underwater noise pollution in other locations has been linked to disturbance and injury. Many marine mammals respond to noise by altering their breathing rates, spending more time underwater before coming up for air, changing the depths or speeds of their dives, shielding their young, changing their vocalization content and durations, and swimming away from the affected area (Richardson et al. 1995). Acute sound intensities may cause marine mammals and other organisms to undergo temporary or permanent hearing loss. The disorientation and hearing loss may account for some cases in which ships collide with marine mammals that are apparently unaware of the approaching vessel. Most strikes occur in coastal waters on the continental shelf, where large marine mammals concentrate to feed. High levels of noise could also affect predation efficiency for marine mammals that use sound to hunt or capture prey. Underwater noise has also been found to negatively affect social behaviors in fish because many species rely on vocalizations when courting potential mates, and most detect sound vibrations that can be used to localize food or avoid predators (Myrberg 1990). In extreme cases, such as air guns used for seismic exploration, extensive damage was reported in laboratory study to the sensory epithelia of fish ears with no subsequent repair or replacement of damaged sensory cells (McCauley et al. 2003).

## Climate Change

Over the next century, climate change is projected to profoundly impact coastal and marine ecosystems on a global scale, with anticipated effects on sea level, temperature, storm intensity and current patterns. At a regional scale, we can anticipate significant shifts in the species composition of ecological communities, seasonal flows in freshwater systems, rates of primary productivity, sea level rise, coastal flooding and erosion, and wind-driven circulation patterns (Scavia et al. 2002). Rising seawater temperatures may give rise to increased algal blooms, major shifts in species distributions, local species extirpations, and increases in pathogenic diseases (Epstein et al. 1993, Harvell et al. 1999). A better understanding of ocean responses to global scale climatic changes is needed in order to improve interpretation of observable ecosystem fluctuations, such as temperature changes, hypoxic events and ocean acidity, that may or may not be directly coupled to climate change.

# State of Sanctuary Resources

This section provides summaries of the conditions and trends within four resource areas: water, habitat, living resources, and maritime archaeological resources. Sanctuary staff and selected outside experts considered a series of questions about each resource area. The set of questions derive from the National Marine Sanctuary System's mission, and a system-wide monitoring framework (National Marine Sanctuary Program 2004) developed to ensure the timely flow of data and information to those responsible for managing and protecting resources in the ocean and coastal zone, and to those that use, depend on, and study the ecosystems encompassed by the sanctuaries. The questions are meant to set the limits of judgments so that responses can be confined to certain reporting categories that will later be compared among all sanctuary sites and combined. Appendix A (Rating Scale for System-Wide Monitoring Questions) clarifies the questions and presents statements that were used to judge the status and assign a corresponding color code on a scale from "good" to "poor." These statements are customized for each question. In addition, symbols are used to indicate trends. Methods for consultation with experts and development of status and trends ratings are described in Appendix B.

This section of the report provides answers to the set of questions for Olympic Coast National Marine Sanctuary. Answers are supported by specific examples of data, investigations, monitoring and observations, and the basis for judgment is provided in the text and summarized in the table for each resource area. Where published or additional information exists, the reader is provided with appropriate references and web links.

## Water Quality Status and Trends

Water quality within the sanctuary is largely representative of natural ocean conditions, with relatively minor influence from human activities at sea and on land. By conventional measures, marine water quality within the sanctuary is not notably compromised. There are very few point sources of pollution in the vicinity, such as sewage outfalls or industrial discharge sites, to degrade water conditions. To date, the sparse human population has limited nonpoint source pollution — the harmful byproducts of everyday activities, such as pathogens from failing septic systems, residues from domestic products, excess nutrients, petroleum combustion byproducts, or hydrocarbons from roads and highways — that might enter the oceanic food web. However, increased sediment loading in rivers from logging, road building and upland development has been a concern for impacts to nearshore habitats.

Although water quality within the sanctuary is currently good, the potential for contamination by petroleum products, pathogens and chemicals is a concern. Four of the five largest oil spills in Washington state history have occurred in or moved into the area now designated as the sanctuary. In the decade before sanctuary designation, two major oil spills released more than 1,230,258 liters (325,000 gallons) of petroleum products that impacted marine ecosystems and human communities on the outer Washington coast. Moreover, naturally occurring harmful algal blooms can elevate the risk of shellfish poisoning. Recently documented, widespread hypoxic conditions in

## Water Quality Status & Trends

| # | Issue | Rating | Basis for Judgment | Description of Findings |
|---|-------|--------|--------------------|--------------------------|
| 1 | Stressors | ? | Hypoxic conditions may be increasing in frequency and spatial extent in nearshore waters. | Selected conditions may preclude full development of living resource assemblages and habitats, but are not likely to cause substantial or persistent declines. |
| 2 | Eutrophic Condition | — | No suspected human influence on harmful algal blooms or eutrophication. | Conditions do not appear to have the potential to negatively affect living resources or habitat quality. |
| 3 | Human Health | — | Naturally occurring harmful algal blooms result in periodic shellfish closures. | Selected conditions that have the potential to affect human health may exist, but human impacts have not been reported. |
| 4 | Human Activities | — | Threat of oil spills from vessels. | Some potentially harmful activities exist, but they do not appear to have had a negative effect on water quality. |

Status: Good   Good/Fair   Fair   Fair/Poor   Poor   Undet.

Trends: Improving (▲), Not Changing (—), Getting Worse (▼), Undetermined Trend (?), Question not applicable (N/A)

nearshore areas off Oregon and part of the Washington coast appear to result from anomalous weather and oceanographic patterns.

The following information summarizes assessments by sanctuary staff and subject area experts of the status and trends pertaining to water quality.

1.  *Are specific or multiple stressors, including chang-ing oceanographic and atmospheric conditions, affecting water quality?* Whereas sanctuary waters are not degraded by persistent chemical contamination, periodic incursion of oxygen-depleted water to continental shelf and nearshore waters has killed organisms in its pathway. Potential and early evidence of linkages between climate change and changing oceanic conditions with these hypoxic events, as well as local effects on toxic algae blooms, increasing water temperature and acidity, all lead to uncertainty about the trends in these stressors.

Oxygen serves a critical role in defining ocean habitats. Deep waters on the continental shelf normally have low oxygen concentrations, and resident organisms are adapted to oxygen levels that can be lethal to animals living in near-surface and nearshore waters. Further depression of oxygen levels near the deep seafloor and movement of oxygen-depleted waters toward shore, however, can stress living communities. Hypoxia (low oxygen levels, or dissolved $O_2$ below 1.4 ml/L) is often associated with high nutrient loading from land-based sources, while off Washington's outer coast it is a function of wind-driven up-welling dynamics and ocean conditions that control the delivery of oxygen-poor, nutrient-rich deep water across the continental shelf (Grantham et al. 2004). Hypoxic conditions severe enough

to cause widespread fish and invertebrate mortality were documented off the Washington and Oregon coasts in 2006. Figure 17 provides data from the sanctuary's monitoring station off Cape Elizabeth showing hypoxic conditions that persisted close to shore for more than two weeks in July 2006. Other invertebrate and fish mortality events have been observed along Washington's coast, for example in 2001 and 2002, but historic records and oxygen monitoring data are not available to definitively link previous mortality events to hypoxic conditions.

A major oceanographic feature off the eastern Pacific Coast, the oxygen minimum zone, is a layer of deep water along the upper continental slope extending to depths greater than 1,000 meters where dissolved oxygen levels are persistently low (Deuser 1975). Analysis of a long-term data set, the 50-year data record from the eastern subarctic Pacific, indicates that deep waters beyond the continental shelf, although normally hypoxic, show trends of increased temperature and lower oxygen (Whitney et al. 2006). As this occurs, deep waters transported across the continental shelf and upwelling toward shore may be increasingly depleted of oxygen and may cause more stress to living resources in the sanctuary.

Grantham et al. (2004) described the development of near-shore hypoxic conditions in the Pacific Northwest as "a novel emergence" that may represent a critical link between climate variability and ecosystem sensitivity to such changes. Although there is some historic evidence that hypoxic conditions have occurred along the Oregon and Washington coasts in the past (Hickey pers. comm.), a comprehensive set of historic data from Oregon's shelf waters indicates that the severity, geographic extent, and duration of hypoxic conditions off Oregon have increased since 2000, and

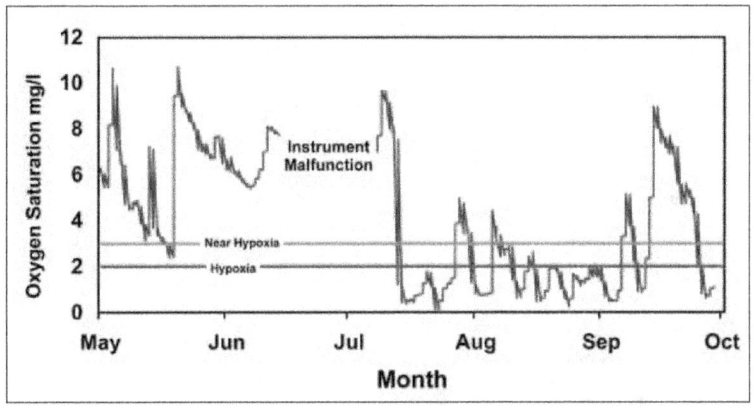

Figure 17. Oxygen data taken concurrently with the July 2006 fish kill first reported by Quinault Natural Resources Department. Oxygen was measured at 1 meter from the bottom at an Olympic Coast sanctuary mooring station off Cape Elizabeth in 15-meter-deep water. Source: OCNMS data

anoxic conditions (water completely devoid of oxygen) had never been recorded before the 2006 event (Chan et al. 2008).

Harmful algal bloom (HAB) events are common in sanctuary waters and can affect wildlife and marine ecosystems, as well as human health. Figure 18 shows the presence and unpredictability of high-domoic acid events at two beaches approximately 40 kilometers (25 miles) apart on the shores of the sanctuary (domoic acid is a toxin produced by one particular type of harmful algae). Some scientists suspect that HABs off the outer coast are increasing in frequency, but long-term records are not available for confirmation.

Recent evidence of increasing seawater acidity (low pH), increases in water temperature, and shifts in oceanographic conditions have been attributed to anthropogenically influenced climate change (Wootton unpublished data, Grantham et al. 2004, Barth et al. 2007, Chan et al. 2008). However, such cause-and-effect linkages are uncertain and will require more data before they are fully accepted.

Existing levels of contaminants (metals, persistent organic pollutants, hydrocarbons, PCBs) are generally at low levels off the Olympic Coast. Measurements of chemical levels in water, sediment and biota in 2003 at 30 stations in the Olympic Coast sanctuary as part of the Environmental Monitoring and Assessment Program indicated good water quality throughout the sanctuary (Partridge 2007).

2. *What is the eutrophic condition of sanctuary waters and how is it changing?* Human-caused eutrophication is not a concern in the sanctuary due to the absence of problematic sources of nutrients, such as population centers or significant municipal discharges in or near the sanctuary. In fact, sampling

in 2003 indicated that conditions for primary production can be limited by a low availability of essential nutrients in summer months off the Washington coast (Partridge 2007). This would suggest that if nutrient supplies were to increase during that time of year, blooms could be triggered. Local inputs of nutrients are not expected to increase significantly, but because long-term datasets and sufficient instrumentation are lacking, there is not information to document a change or trend in nutrient concentrations in sanctuary waters.

The Juan de Fuca Eddy system is a naturally occurring, seasonally intensified water circulation feature covering northern sanctuary waters (Figure 19). It covers a broad region beginning roughly 70 kilometers west of Cape Flattery and contains elevated macronutrients levels. Nutrients in this system are derived primarily from upwelling of nutrient-rich deep waters from the California Undercurrent, combined with lesser contributions from the Strait of Juan de Fuca outflow (MacFadyen et al. 2008). The feature's retentive circulation patterns and nutrient supply promote high primary productivity within the eddy, and periodic advection of these water masses toward shore has been identified as a trigger for HABs in sanctuary waters (Foreman et al. 2007, MacFadyen et al. 2005). Consequently, HABs in the sanctuary are currently considered natural phenomena that are not enhanced by anthropogenic inputs of nutrients or eutrophic conditions.

3. *Do sanctuary waters pose risks to human health and how are they changing?* The main risk to human health posed by sanctuary waters is through consumption of tainted shellfish. Levels of naturally occurring biotoxins in excess of action levels to protect human health have been detected once or

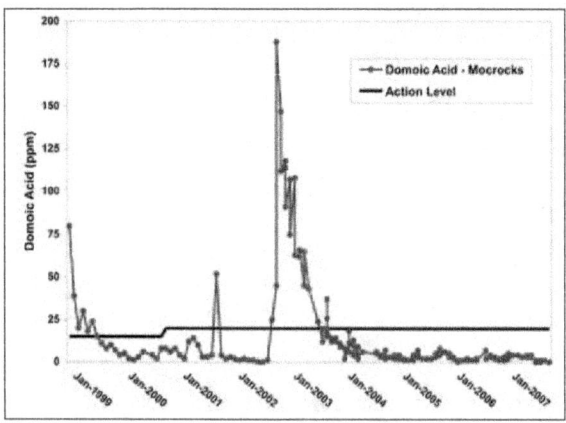
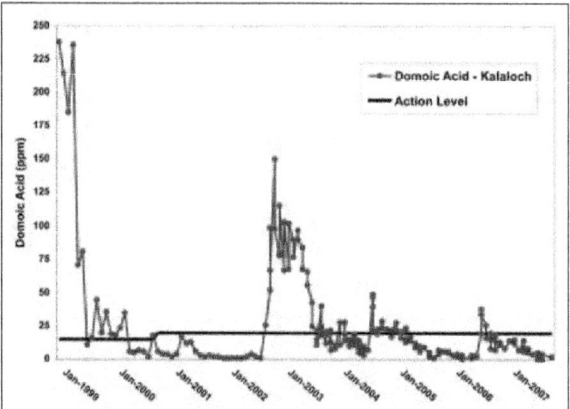

Figure 18. Domoic acid levels in razor clams from the Kalaloch and Mocrocks (near Moclips River) razor clam management areas, where large recreational razor clam fisheries occur. Shellfish harvesting is closed when tissue levels exceed the action level. Source: WDFW data

twice a year, on average, over the past 16 years, but the limited historical record precludes the identification of any long-term trend in the frequency of toxin level spikes.

Shellfish on the outer Washington coast is normally safe for human consumption, yet during HAB events filter feeding organisms, such as hard-shelled clams and mussels, can concentrate toxins produced by some species of plankton, rendering them toxic to consumers. Routine monitoring is conducted at selected locations by coastal tribes and Washington state, and shellfish harvest closures are enacted when concentrations exceed action levels for protection of human health. Rapid detection techniques are being sought to enhance the ability to monitor for toxins. Risk of human exposure remains, however, because it can be difficult to reach all subsistence and recreational harvesters on this remote coast.

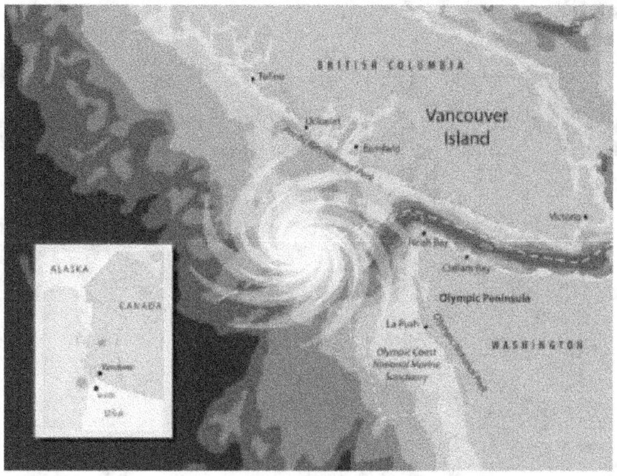

Figure 19. The Juan de Fuca Eddy (also called the Big Eddy) is west of the Strait of Juan de Fuca and spans the international boundary between U.S. and Canadian waters. Image: Canadian Parks and Wilderness Society

For centuries, consumers of bivalves in the Pacific Northwest have known about paralytic shellfish poisoning (PSP), which is caused by saxitoxins produced by dinoflagellates. In 1991, domoic acid, a neurotoxin produced by diatoms in the genus *Pseudo-nitzschia* that causes amnesic shellfish poisoning (ASP), was first detected in clams on Washington's outer coast. High levels of either toxin have led to multiple restrictions on the popular recreational razor clam harvest and commercial harvest by local Indian tribes (Figure 18). For the shoreline adjacent to the sanctuary, Washington State Department of Health records since 1991 indicate 14 shellfish harvest closures based on ASP and nine closures based on PSP concerns. The state health department has received no reports of shellfish poisoning on the outer coast since 1991, although exposures (but no deaths) have been reported from other areas in Washington.

As discussed above, harmful algal blooms in the Olympic Coast sanctuary are naturally occurring phenomena. With more intensive monitoring in recent years, there is a perception that blooms have increased in frequency. However, there are insufficient data to confirm a trend because monitoring began only in the 1990s and shellfish poisoning may have been misdiagnosed in the past (Juan de Fuca Eddy Steering Committee 2004, Train-

er 2005, Trainer and Suddeson 2005). If HABs are increasing in frequency, contributing factors may include increased advection of offshore waters shoreward as a result of reduced volume of the Columbia Plume (due to dams and water removals) and altered wind and current patterns due to climate change (Juan de Fuca Eddy Steering Committee 2004, Hickey pers. comm.).

Limited bacterial monitoring in marine waters is conducted by the state health department with assistance from coastal tribes in order to assess human health risks in shellfish harvest areas (Washington State Department of Health 2008). In addition, Surfrider's Blue Water Task Force volunteers monitored five additional sites in the sanctuary during 2003-2005 (http://www.surfrider.org/whatwedo3c.asp). These data indicate there are no significant concerns regarding bacteria such as fecal coliform, *E. coli* and *Enterococcus* in the sanctuary waters.

4. *What are the levels of human activities that may influence water quality and how are they changing?*
The high volume of marine traffic, particularly through northern sanctuary waters, introduces the threat of catastrophic injury to marine resources from an oil spill. This threat is persistent but not changing significantly because vessel management procedures and preventative measures have been implemented, and vessel traffic volumes have been stable in recent years.

The potential for a large-volume oil spill is generally considered the greatest threat to the sanctuary's water quality — a low-probability but high-impact threat. The northern area of the sanctuary lies at the western Strait of Juan de Fuca, the major passage for the incoming and outgoing shipping traffic that lead to the Pacific Northwest's major ports: Seattle, Tacoma and Vancouver, British Columbia. Large commercial vessels, including oil tankers and freighters with large fuel capacity, transit through and near the sanctuary daily, creating a persistent and elevated risk of accidental and catastrophic release of toxic products. An estimated 5.7 billion liters (1.5 billion gallons) of oil are transported through the area each year. Tanker and container traffic occurs daily through all seasons and weather, with about 5,500 freighters and 1,400 tankers transiting the Strait of Juan de

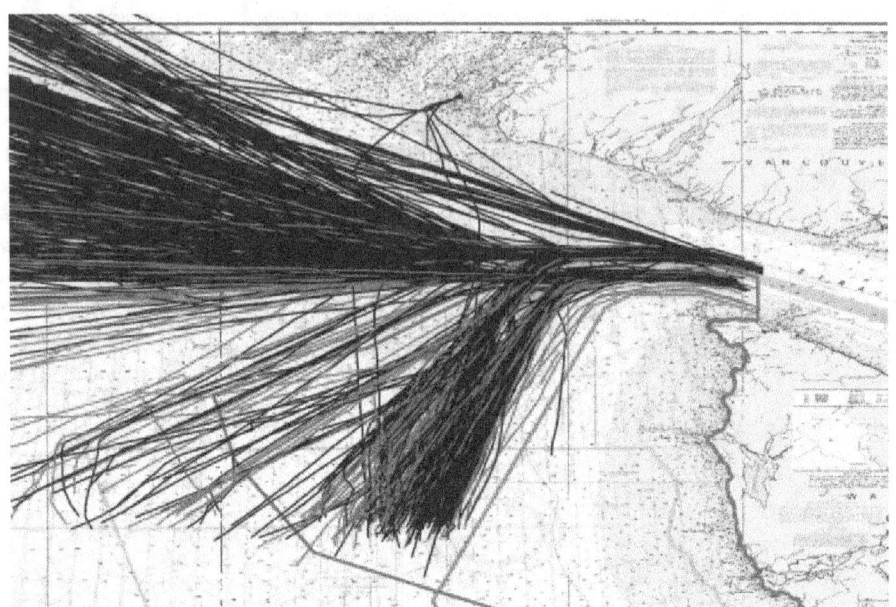

Figure 20. Track lines from large commercial vessels transiting the western Strait of Juan de Fuca in June 2007. Purple lines are tanker traffic. Darker lines are freighter traffic. The light blue line is the sanctuary boundary, and the red line marks the Area-To-Be-Avoided. Source: OCNMS

Fuca in 2006 (data from Marine Exchange of Seattle) (Figure 20). Vessel entry and transit data for the Strait of Juan de Fuca compiled by Washington State Department of Ecology indicate the number of large non-tank vessels (less than 300 gross tons; cargo, passenger, and commercial fishing industry vessels) has decreased by about 17 percent in the past decade, while the number of tank ship transits has increased by 50 percent (from 547 in 1998 to 820 in 2007). Overall, the number of large vessels transiting the Strait may have increased over the past few decades, but has been stable in the past decade.

In the previous century, weak environmental regulations allowed logging and road building practices to damage freshwater habitats and riparian systems in the Pacific Northwest. Rivers and creeks in logged watersheds discharging into marine waters of the outer Washington coast carried elevated burdens of suspended materials that increased turbidity of nearshore marine waters. Although definitive documentation is not available, these conditions may have inhibited growth of macroalgae in areas near river mouths (Devinny and Volse 1978, Dayton et al. 1992, Norse 1994). Logging remains a major industry on the Olympic Peninsula, and whereas improved regulatory oversight of logging practices may have led to reduced inputs of fine particulates from recent harvest areas, effects from historic activities continue to impact freshwater systems flowing into the sanctuary.

Sanctuary waters are protected from impacts of ballast water discharge by regulations that prohibit discharge within 50 nautical miles (93 kilometers) of shore. The cruise ship industry is rapidly expanding in the Pacific Northwest, with passenger numbers increasing from 120,000 to 781,000 through the Port of Seattle between 2000 and 2007 (WDOE 2008). In 2007, the industry agreed to avoid discharge of biosolids (i.e., sewage sludge) in sanctuary waters. These ships can, however, discharge treated sewage, graywater and blackwater in the sanctuary, in accordance with state and federal law. Cruise ships generate an average of 79,500 liters (21,000 gallons) per day per vessel, but the majority have advanced wastewater treatment systems (EPA 2007).

Coastal development adjacent to the sanctuary is sparse, with a few small population centers on tribal reservation lands and growing residential development along the southern shores of the sanctuary. State and county development regulations should minimize impacts of the growing coastal populations on marine water quality, but this remains a potential threat because of ever increasing pressure for coastal development.

## Habitat Status and Trends

Marine habitats of the sanctuary extend from the intertidal, which is accessible daily during low tides, to the depths of submarine canyons that are only seen by humans via submarines, sensors, or lenses on remotely or autonomously operated vehicles. The sanctuary covers a large area, with physically and biologically complex habitats. Exploration and habitat mapping involves carefully planned and costly

### Habitat Status & Trends

| # | Issue | Rating | Basis for Judgment | Description of Findings |
|---|-------|--------|--------------------|--------------------------|
| 5 | Abundance/ Distribution | – | Reduction in habitat complexity by bottom-tending gear; short-term impacts from fishing gear and cable installation. | Selected habitat loss or alteration has taken place, precluding full development of living resource assemblages, but it is unlikely to cause substantial or persistent degradation in living resources or water quality. |
| 6 | Structure | ? | Damage by bottom-tending gear in some deep biogenic habitats. | Selected habitat loss or alteration may inhibit the development of living resources, and may cause measurable but not severe declines in living resources or water quality. |
| 7 | Contaminants | – | Prior studies indicate low levels of contaminants. | Contaminants do not appear to have the potential to negatively affect living resources or water quality. |
| 8 | Human Activities | ▲ | Decrease in bottom trawling and presumably impacts to hard-bottom habitats. | Selected activities have resulted in measurable habitat impacts, but evidence suggests effects are localized, not widespread. |

Status: Good  Good/Fair  Fair  Fair/Poor  Poor  Undet.

Trends: Improving (▲), Not Changing (—), Getting Worse (▼), Undetermined Trend (?), Question not applicable (N/A)

surveys from large vessels using sophisticated technology. Thus far, the sanctuary has completed detailed habitat mapping for about 25 percent of its seafloor, while information on remaining areas lacks resolution and specificity (Figure 21). As a result, generalizations about the sanctuary's habitats are difficult to make. The following discussion focuses on available information wherever possible, but also includes speculative analysis based on habitats from similar areas and impacts to these habitats documented at other locations.

The Olympic Coast sanctuary's habitats, similar to its waters, are relatively uncontaminated by chemicals introduced by human activities. Intertidal and nearshore habitats are not considered substantially altered or degraded. Underwater noise pollution and marine debris do compromise habitat quality, but their impacts in the sanctuary are not well-documented. The most significant concern relates to several decades of intensive efforts by fisheries using bottom-contact gear. At locations where biologically structured habitats existed on the sanctuary seafloor, it is likely they have been altered by fishing practices, except perhaps in the roughest of terrain that fishermen avoided. Recovery of biologically structured habitats is expected to occur very slowly, even in the absence of future pressures.

The following information provides an assessment by sanctuary staff and subject area experts of the status and trends pertaining to the current state of marine habitats.

5. *What are the abundance and distribution of major habitat types and how are they changing?* This question focuses on changes to the type and physical composition of marine habitats, whereas Question 6 focuses on biologically structured habitats. Past or ongoing modification of habitat types (e.g., conversion of coastal marsh into upland) from extensive physical disturbance or alterations to physical forces is not a concern in the sanctuary. Some reduction to the physical complexity of deep seafloor habitats, however, has resulted from extensive bottom trawling activity over the past half-century. Recent fishery management measures have limited bottom trawl efforts in areas where the seafloor is most susceptible to physical alteration, so future alteration of habitat from this activity is likely to be minimal, as long as trawl area closures remain in effect.

With limited exceptions, nearshore and intertidal habitats in the sanctuary are remarkably undisturbed by human use and development that has modified habitats in more urbanized areas, such as shoreline armoring, wetlands alteration, dredging, and land-based construction. The remote location, low levels of human habitation, protections provided by the wilderness designation of Olympic National Park's coast, and restricted access to tribal reservations have allowed these coastal habitats to persist largely intact. At the few locations where shore-line armoring has been employed or where human visitation has focused on intertidal areas for food collection and recreation, impacts do not appear to be dramatic or widespread (Erickson and Wullschleger 1998; Erickson 2005).

Data on habitats of the deeper waters of the sanctuary are limited. Only 25 percent of the sanctuary has been characterized using modern, high-resolution acoustic and imaging methods (Intelmann 2006, Bowlby et al. 2008). Low-resolution surveys have revealed a generally wide and featureless continental shelf in the southern portion of the sanctuary dominated by soft substrates with areas of rock outcrop and spires, and the Quinault Canyon. High-resolution mapping may reveal more complex features along the shelf than presently indicated. The northern portion of the sanctuary is dominated by the Juan de Fuca Canyon and trough, complex, glacially carved features containing a mixture of soft sediments, with significant cobble and boulder patches and scattered large glacial erratics deposited during ice retreat. Most of the trough, the shallower extensions of the canyon closer to the Strait of Juan de Fuca, has been mapped using high-resolution methods. Comprehensive surveys with both multi-beam and side-scan techniques have not been completed for the Nitinat, Juan de Fuca, and Quinault canyons.

The most significant physical alteration of sanctuary habitats, besides that caused by natural forces, is likely to have resulted from commercial fishing with bottom trawl gear. Known physical impacts of bottom trawl gear on seafloor habitats from similar areas, in combination with historic fishing patterns in the sanctuary, are evidence that such habitat alterations have likely occurred. Bottom trawl gear is known to reduce complexity and alter the physical structure of seafloor habitats (NRC 2002). Bottom trawling can smooth sedi-

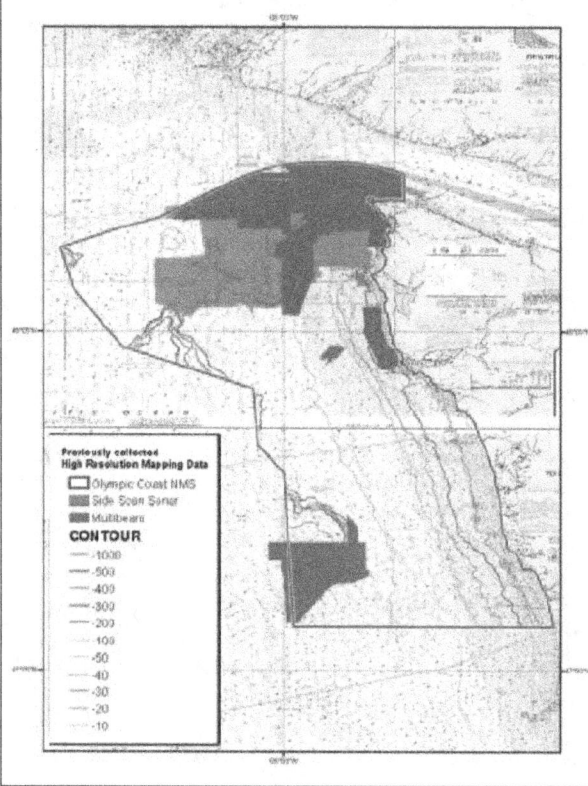

Figure 21. Areas where high-resolution seafloor habitat mapping has been completed by NOAA in Olympic Coast National Marine Sanctuary. Source: OCNMS

mentary bedforms, such as sand waves, reduce bottom roughness, alter the size distribution of surficial features, impact biogenic structures, and roll and move boulders on the seafloor (Auster et al. 1996, Auster and Langton 1999, Whatling and Norse 1999, Thrush and Dayton 2002). Moreover, monitoring by the sanctuary has shown that acute and localized seafloor impacts from submarine cable installations result in short-term habitat disturbance in soft sediments and more persistent physical disturbance in hard substrates. Cable trenching, however, covers a very small portion of the sanctuary seafloor. Monitoring by the sanctuary has also revealed rolled and displaced boulders as a result of cable trenching and bottom-contact commercial fishing gear. Dredging, another fishing technique that causes acute physical disruption of the seafloor, has not been widely employed in the sanctuary.

NOAA Fisheries Service statistics indicate that the northern waters of the sanctuary were one of the most intensively fished bottom trawl areas along the West Coast of the United States in the later half of the 1900s (Shoji 1999). Groundfish landings in Washington, the majority of which were from bottom trawlers, averaged 30 to 40 million pounds annually from the mid-1950s through about 1980. To put this into perspective, non-tribal bottom trawl landings into Washington have averaged about 7 million pounds per year in recent years (2004-06), which represents a decline of about 80 percent since the earlier time period. The number of vessels participating in the fishery shows similar trends. About 100 trawl vessels landed and sold groundfish on the Washington coast (excluding Puget Sound) between the late 1970s and early 1990s (Shoji 1999). As a result of a federal buy-back program in 2003 and attrition in the fishery, in some cases, as a direct result of increasing fishing restrictions, the number of non-tribal trawl vessels landing into Washington has declined to less than 10 vessels per year, which represents about a 90 percent decrease from historical participation levels. Another statistic relevant to potential habitat impact is trawl effort. The total hours of trawler fishing effort on the outer coast averaged about 10,000 hours per year between 1989 and 1997 (Shoji 1999), yet a subsequent decline in the amount of trawl hours has also occurred as the number of vessels has decreased, coupled with a general reduction in trawl trip limits for target species. While Washington bottom trawl fisher-

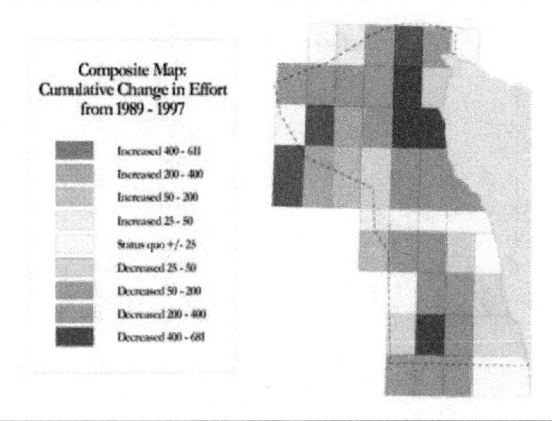

Figure 22. Composite map of overall change in bottom trawl effort by WDFW block area over 1989-1997. Source: Shoji 1999

men typically used moderate-sized vessels (e.g., less than 30.5 meters or 100 feet length), there was an especially high-impact fishery practiced in deeper waters for more than two decades. Beginning in 1966, a large Soviet fleet of factory trawlers began fishing off the U.S. coasts of California, Oregon and Washington. The vessels were large stern ramp trawlers exceeding 76 meters (250 feet) in length using large gear that fished mostly on the continental shelf and upper slope at depths ranging from about 91 to 220 meters (300 to 720 feet). Their efforts continued until 1991, when all commercial fishing by foreign vessels was excluded from waters within 200 nautical miles (370 kilometers) of the U.S. coastline.

Although the manner in which data were collected in the past makes it difficult to map precisely the level of bottom trawl effort by area, there clearly has been significant interaction between the fishery and the sanctuary seafloor for several decades. Although bottom trawl effort in different areas has changed over time, analysis of Washington Department of Fish and Wildlife (WDFW) commercial trawl logbooks between 1989 and 1997 indicates that trawling occurred widely throughout the sanctuary during this period (Figure 22). There is also an indication of increased trawling pressure within the individual blocks depicted in Figure 21, where the number of blocks with greater than 120 tows per year increased from zero to 11 for the time intervals of 1991-1993 and 1997-1999, respectively (data compiled from NRC 2002). Moreover, large footrope gear (i.e., footrope greater than eight inches in diameter) that allows trawlers to access rockier areas by bouncing the bottom of the trawl net over larger obstructions without tearing nets, was not restricted West Coast-wide until 2000 (PFMC 2005). In recent years, fish-

ery management measures that restrict footrope gear size and limit areas open to trawlers have focused trawl effort more toward soft seafloor substrates where gear impacts on the physical habitat are less of a concern. Off of Washington, WDFW has had a five-inch footrope restriction on non-tribal trawling in state waters (within three nautical miles or 5.5 kilometers of shore) since 1996; WDFW then followed up with a complete prohibition on bottom trawl gear in state waters in 2000. More recent designation of Essential Fish Habitat and Rockfish Conservation Areas, which restrict bottom trawl fishing by non-tribal commercial vessels, and Non-Trawl Rockfish Conservation Areas that restrict longline and pot gear, also reduces seafloor impacts in the sanctuary by non-tribal fishers. These measures are discussed in more detail in the Response to Pressures section of this report. Although detailed information on historic and current conditions in the sanctuary's deep seafloor habitats is limited, the degree and extent of alteration to the physical complexity of these habitats resulting from past bottom trawling activity are cause for concern, based on evidence from other locations in both the Pacific and Atlantic (Auster and Langton 1999, NRC 2002, Thrush and Dayton 2002). The most significant threat, however, is the impact of these damages to the distribution and abundance of biologically structured habitats on the sanctuary seafloor (see Question 6).

6. *What is the condition of biologically structured habitats and how is it changing?* Intertidal and nearshore habitats structured by living or once-living organisms are intact and thriving in the sanctuary. Of concern are biogenic habitats in deeper areas of the sanctuary that are presumed to have been degraded by extensive practice of bottom trawl and longline fisheries. The trend is undetermined because these habitats may not recover quickly or may never re-establish to their original composition, and recovery can occur only where bottom contact gear is prohibited.

Biologically structured habitats in rocky intertidal areas include macroalgae and invertebrate communities (e.g., mussel beds) that provide micro-habitats for many species of invertebrates and fish. Monitoring conducted by Olympic National Park since 1989 indicates that these habitats are healthy and do not appear to be changing substantially in response to human influences. Large-scale disturbances related primarily to extreme winter weather cause periodic damage to mussel beds (Paine and Levin 1981). Coastal ecologists have begun to design studies to better detect changes that may result from ef-

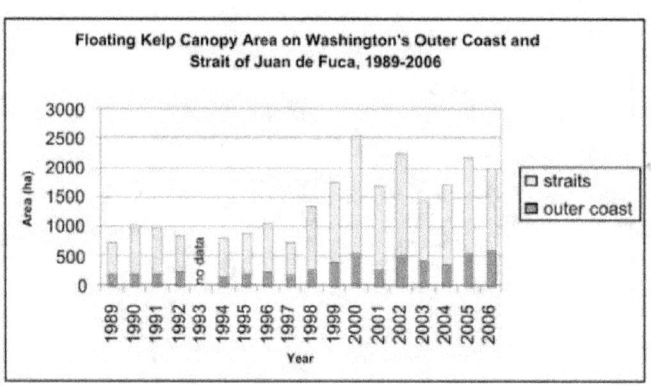

Figure 23. Annual floating kelp canopy area since 1989 along the Washington coast and the Strait of Juan de Fuca. Source: WDNR data

fects of global climate change, such as sea level rise, reduced pH, increasing temperatures, and changes in storm frequency and magnitude. Local trends in these parameters are uncertain, however, and no definitive results have yet been published.

In nearshore areas, canopy kelp beds form a productive, physically complex and protected habitat with a rich biological community association of fish, invertebrates and sea otters. The first historical record for Washington kelp occurred in 1912 (Rigg 1915) as part of the war effort to assess potential sources of potash. Annual monitoring and quantification of the floating kelp canopy has been conducted since 1989 by the Washington Department of Natural Resources and in collaboration with the sanctuary since 1995. Although the canopy changes every year, these kelp beds are generally considered stable. In fact, the area covered by floating kelp has been increasing along the outer coast and western portion of the Strait of Juan de Fuca (Figure 23; Berry et al. 2005; http://www1.dnr.wa.gov/htdocs/aqr/nshr/pdf/floating_kelpbed.pdf). This increase may be due in part to a growing population of sea otters and subsequent decline in grazing sea urchins or may be influenced by changes in oceanographic conditions. In contrast, extensive logging of the Olympic Peninsula, an area of very high rainfall, has markedly increased sediment loads in rivers in the past. Long-term residents along the coast have noted a reduction in kelp beds near river mouths, which may have been associated with siltation of nearshore habitat and reduced light penetration (Chris Morganroth III, personal communication in Norse 1994).

Some deepwater corals found off the Pacific Coast are designated as "structure forming" because they provide vertical structure above the seafloor that serves as habitat for other invertebrate and fish species (Whitmire and Clarke 2007). Other emergent epifauna, such as sponges, hydroids and bryozoans,

also provide living habitat for invertebrates and fishes. These organisms are vulnerable to damage from bottom contact fishing gear, and because many have slow growth and recruitment rates, damage can be long-lasting (Auster and Langton 1999, Whatling and Norse 1999, NRC 2002, Thrush and Dayton 2002). Information on the historic distribution and condition of habitat-forming corals in the sanctuary is extremely limited, based on observations compiled from NOAA Fisheries trawl surveys from which identification of invertebrates was very limited particularly prior to 1980 (Whitmire and Clarke 2007) and occasional observations by West Coast research institutions (Etnoyer and Morgan 2003). These data, augmented by video surveys conducted more recently by the sanctuary in limited areas, indicate the presence of several habitat-forming species. The paucity of data is indicated by the first discovery in 2004 of *Lophelia pertusa* in the sanctuary (Hyland et al. 2005), a species with high potential as a biogenic habitat producer (Whitmire and Clarke 2007). Surveys conducted since then have documented additional living and dead colonies of *L. pertusa* and several other species of corals and sponges in the sanctuary (Brancato et al. 2007). Analysis of seafloor habitat data used for Essential Fish Habitat (EFH) designation indicates that approximately 6 percent of the sanctuary is hard substrate with potential to host biologically structured habitat (Figure 24). Of this, 29 percent lies within the Olympic 2 EFH conservation area (see Figure 35, page 46). Recent surveys by Olympic Coast sanctuary researchers have documented corals and other biologically structured habitat in other areas, which indicates this analysis may underestimate the historic or current distribution of biologically structured habitat.

Of all fishing gear types used in the region, bottom trawls have the highest ranking (in terms of severity and extent of damage) for potential impacts to deep corals (Morgan and Chuendpagdee 2003). A single pass of a bottom trawl was shown to have significant impacts on corals in Alaska (Krieger 2001). Bottom trawls are followed in severity by bottom longlines. Longline gear can travel significant distances over the seafloor, particularly during retrieval, snaring or undercutting emergent structures (Whitmire and Clarke 2007). Several recent man-

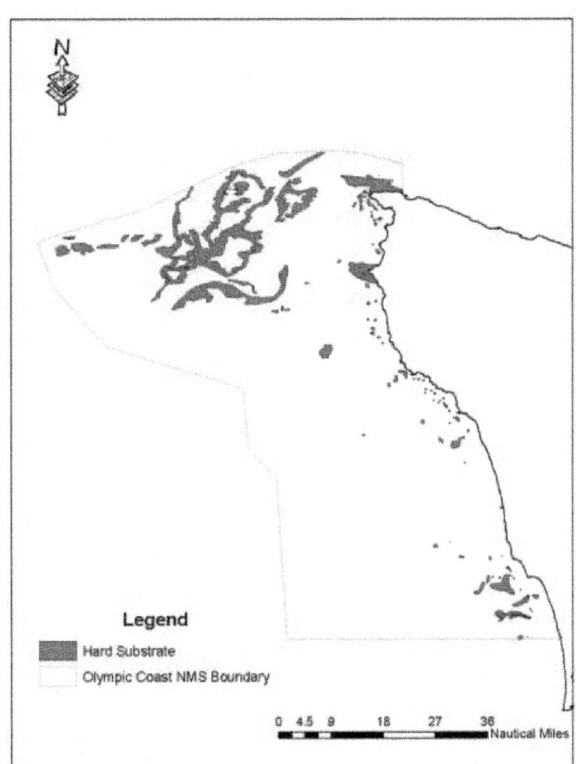

Figure 24. Potential historic distribution of biologically structured habitat associated with hard substrate in the Olympic Coast sanctuary. Source: NOAA data

**Legend**

Hard Substrate

Olympic Coast NMS Boundary

0  4.5  9       18       27       36
Nautical Miles

agement measures implemented through the Pacific Fisheries Management Council for non-tribal commercial fisheries, such as footrope size restrictions, EFH designations, vessel buy-back programs, and Rockfish Conservation Area designations restricting use of trawl and non-trawl gear, will reduce ongoing impacts to such habitats.

The condition of the sanctuary's biologically structured habitats prior to modern fishing activities may never be known. However, we do know that bottom trawl and longline fisheries have been widely practiced in the sanctuary for many decades, likely over all but the roughest of seafloor habitats. We also know that the sanctuary waters contain hard-bottom habitats that can support biogenic structures that are susceptible to damages from these activities. Consequently, we believe it is reasonable to assume that where trawl and longline fisheries have occurred on deep-sea biogenic habitats, it is likely they have been degraded and may not quickly recover. For example, growth rate studies of red tree coral from Alaska indicate recovery of fish habitat from trawl impacts may take 100 years or more (Andrews et al. 2002).

Intensive survey efforts will be required to determine the extent of detectable damage, and the rate of recovery can only be determined within areas where these practices are no longer allowed.

7. *What are the contaminant concentrations in sanctuary habitats and how are they changing?* Sediment contamination levels (i.e., heavy metals and organic pollutants) in the Olympic Coast sanctuary are generally low and do not appear to be increasing. In 30 sediment samples taken in 2003 as part of the West Coast Environmental Monitoring and Assessment Program, there were no PCBs, DDT, or other chlorinated pesticides detected (Partridge 2007). Polycyclic aromatic hydrocarbons (PAHs; found in oils and byproducts of petroleum combustion) and metals were found in the sediment throughout the sanctuary, but no concentrations exceeded Washington state sediment quality standards (WDOE 1995). At one location, a sediment quality guideline predictive of toxicity called the Effects Range-Low (ERL) was exceeded for silver, and at four locations the ERL was exceeded for chromium. The ERL is a concentration correlated with a low likelihood of toxicity to biological organisms (Long et al. 1995, O'Connor 2004). Anthropogenic sources for these metals are not known, but given the low level of human development along the shoreline, these conditions are not likely to change in the near future. Lost lead fishing weights may be a contaminant source, particularly if ingested by wildlife, but there have been no investigations to assess this risk in sanctuary waters.

Concentrations of contaminants in tissues can provide an integrated measure of bioavailability of compounds that are present at low or variable levels in the marine system. Chemical concentrations were recently measured in a variety of invertebrates and sea otters for a study of sea otter health (Brancato et al. 2006), the West Coast Environmental Monitoring and Assessment Program, and for NOAA's Status and Trends, Mussel Watch Program. Contaminant concentrations were found to be low in all organisms, with very few exceptions.

Two potentially significant sources of chemical contaminants in the sanctuary include petroleum releases and atmospheric deposition. Physical evidence, such as tar balls on beaches and oil sheens on water, are occasionally noted in the sanctuary, but persistent and widespread contamination from petroleum has not been documented outside of major oil spills, the most recent of which occurred in 1991. Atmospheric sources of contaminants, however, are a growing regional concern associated with rapid industrialization of Southeast Asia (Wilkening et al. 2000), but the most significant impacts are anticipated in terrestrial systems.

**8. *What are the levels of human activities that may influence habitat quality and how are they changing?***

Bottom-tending fishing gear has been employed widely throughout the sanctuary for many decades. Where this has occurred, biologically structured habitat that may have existed is likely to have been degraded. Moreover, diversity of organisms that live in the surface sediment layer, an important element in the seafloor food chain, can be reduced by bottom trawling (Collie et al. 1997; OCNMS unpublished data). Recent fisheries management measures have reduced the potential for further impacts to these habitats by reducing fishing effort and restricting areas where bottom trawling is practiced by non-tribal commercial fishers. Strengthened regulation of land use in watersheds and shoreline areas and management of visitor use in intertidal areas should improve protection of intertidal and nearshore habitats. As a result, it is expected that impacts to sanctuary habitats are decreasing, in general.

The primary activity affecting the deepwater habitats of the sanctuary is bottom-contact fisheries. As noted under Question 5, the bottom trawl effort has significantly declined in comparison to historical levels. Also, the area subject to commercial trawling has been significantly reduced in the sanctuary through designation of permanent closures of groundfish Essential Fish Habitat and the creation of Rockfish Conservation Areas, where trawlers are excluded for the next several decades while key overfished rockfish stocks rebuild, as well as attrition of the fleet resulting in a reduction in bottom trawl effort (Figure 25). Requirements for use of small footrope gear also limits trawling to areas of low "roughness," which tend to be seafloor substrates, such as sand, mud and gravel, where habitat is less degraded by bottom contact gear. If these area and gear restrictions remain in place over time, biogenic structures may improve, though with their low reproductive rates, slow growth rates and patchy distribution of source material, recovery may take decades (Andrews 2002, Etnoyer and Morgan 2003, Morgan et al. 2005, Whitmire and Clarke 2007).

The sanctuary's boundaries include intertidal areas of Olympic National Park where habitat quality can be affected by harvesting and trampling by visitors. Park visitation rates have been relatively stable over the past decade, but the shoreline remains a popular destination, with most visits focused near the few access points where roads or trails approach the coast. Shoreline harvesting by non-tribal visitors is not common, yet evidence of destructive harvest practices, such as boulders denuded for fishing bait collection, can be seen, particularly at easily accessible locations. An exception is the popular razor clam harvest at Kalaloch and Mocrocks beaches, an activity that does not damage the high-energy, sandy beaches where razor clams live. Lo-

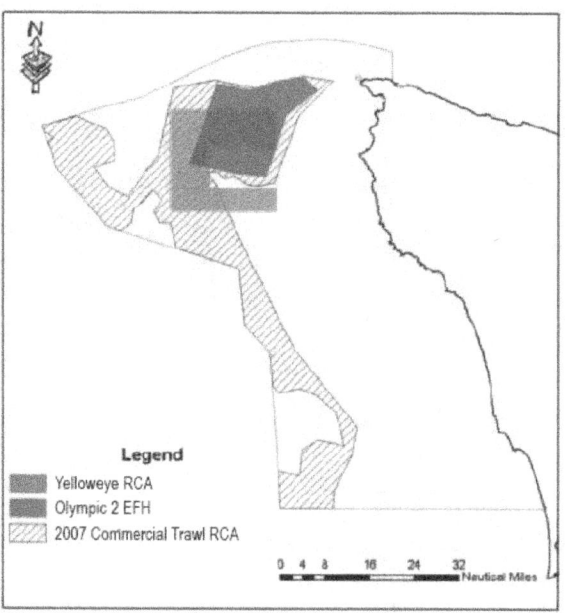

Figure 25. Groundfish Essential Fish Habitat and rockfish conservation areas mapped with OCNMS boundaries. Source: NOAA

calized areas of habitat damage have been caused by fish bait harvesting (Erickson and Wullschleger 1998), but regulations have been implemented to minimize this activity. The park plans to implement harvest closure on approximately 30 percent of the shoreline, which will further reduce the pressure experienced at selected mixed gravel/cobble and rocky intertidal habitats (ONP 2008). Trampling and intertidal exploration may degrade intertidal habitats in some areas, but substantial impacts have not been documented (Erickson 2005).

Marine debris may be an increasing problem for the sanctuary, as has been demonstrated elsewhere. For example, the Ocean Conservancy's monitoring program documented more than a 5 percent increase in debris per year in the United States from 1999 through 2005 (Ocean Conservancy 2007). Wildlife impacts from floating marine debris, such as entanglement and ingestion, have been documented in other areas and are assumed to occur off the Washington coast. Recent cleanup efforts on the Olympic Coast have removed significant quantities of marine debris from beaches — an estimated 24 tons in 2007 during a two-day clean up event — yet debris is continuously deposited on the shores. The decline in nearshore fishing effort and increasing expense of fishing gear might reduce abandonment of fishing gear in the sanctuary. Surveys in limited portions of the sanctuary have revealed few derelict nets in nearshore areas near Cape Flattery. Abandoned crab pots remain a problem along the coast, while in deeper areas abandoned longline gear and netting is likely to remain for many years because removal methods are not cost effective.

Land use in upland areas also has the potential to negatively impact nearshore habitats. Chief among these activities has been timber harvest in upland areas, with consequent alteration of water runoff and sediment transport regimes in rivers and nearshore areas. Road building and maintenance, runoff from roads and the development and maintenance of recreational facilities (e.g., campgrounds) and coastal residences all have potential to degrade nearshore habitats and water quality. Coastal development is increasing along the southern shore of the sanctuary. Although stronger regulation of forestry and construction practices is intended to minimize impacts to marine areas, monitoring for relevant parameters in freshwater inputs to sanctuary waters is not conducted routinely.

The U.S. Navy has historically trained and operated off the Washington coast, as described in the sanctuary's original EIS (NOAA 1993). The Navy's research and testing activities involving non-weaponized technologies, as well as their fleet training activities, currently are being evaluated for effects of existing activities and the associated environment in EIS documents. The Navy has proposed significant expansion in the area and extent of research and testing operations in the sanctuary. Although only non-weaponized technologies would be tested, an increase in Navy activity or areas of operation, if not properly controlled, could have potential to disturb the seabed, introduce pollutants associated with test systems, and produce sound energy that could negatively alter the acoustic environment within the sanctuary.

Underwater noise can act as pollution for acoustically oriented organisms, such as some whale and fish species, and can degrade the underwater habitat. The main source of anthropogenic noise within sanctuary waters is vessel traffic, with some contribution from military activities. The establishment of the Area To Be Avoided (ATBA) and high level of compliance by the commercial shipping industry suggests that the risk of pollution and acoustic impacts associated with shipping are reduced in the southern and nearshore portions of the sanctuary where vessel traffic is directed offshore. In northern sanctuary waters, convergence of Pacific Rim shipping routes into the western Strait of Juan de Fuca, vessel traffic lanes and ATBA boundaries all concentrate large vessels (see Figures 20 and 31) in an area where marine mammal density is relatively high (Calambokidis et al. 2004). Stable levels of shipping traffic in the northern sanctuary over the past five years suggest that noise from ships may remain relatively constant in the near future.

## Living Resources Status and Trends

The living resources of the sanctuary are composed of a wide array of species organized into several ecological communities, including intertidal, nearshore, pelagic and benthic. Community structure is shaped by species-species interactions, such as competition and

### Living Resources Status & Trends

| # | Issue | Rating | Basis for Judgment | Description of Findings |
|---|-------|--------|--------------------|-----------------------|
| 9 | Biodiversity | ? | Ecosystem-level impacts caused by historical depletion of fish, high-order predators, and keystone species. | Selected biodiversity loss may inhibit full community development and function, and may cause measurable but not severe degradation of ecosystem integrity. |
| 10 | Extracted Species | ▲ | Overexploitation of some groundfish species has led to wide area closures to rebuild fish stocks. | Extraction may inhibit full community development and function, and may cause measurable but not severe degradation of ecosystem integrity. |
| 11 | Non-Indigenous Species | ▼ | Invasive *Sargassum* and tunicate distrubutions are expanding. | Non-indigenous species exist, precluding full community development and function, but are unlikely to cause substantial or persistent degradation of ecosystem integrity. |
| 12 | Key Species Status | ? | Populations of Common Murres, sea otters and numerous rockfish reduced from historic levels, with differing recovery rates. | The reduced abundance of selected keystone species may inhibit full community development and function, and may cause measurable but not severe degradation of ecosystem integrity; or selected key species are at reduced levels, but recovery is possible. |
| 13 | Key Species Condition | ? | Diseases detected in sea otters. | The condition of selected key resources is not optimal, perhaps precluding full ecological function, but substantial or persistent declines are not expected. |
| 14 | Human Activities | ▲ | Commercial and recreational fishing pressure has decreased. | Selected activities have resulted in measurable living resource impacts, but evidence suggests effects are localized, not widespread. |

Status: | Good | Good/Fair | Fair | Fair/Poor | Poor | Undet.

Trends: Improving (▲), Not Changing (—), Getting Worse (▼), Undetermined Trend (?), Question not applicable (N/A)

predation, and physical factors like disturbance, upwelling and temperature. Connections between communities are complex when considering that species can move between habitats at various stages of their life history, or even on a daily basis while foraging or seeking shelter. There are knowledge gaps in the dynamics of ecological communities, and these are areas of active and proposed scientific investigation.

Given the complexity of community types and the diversity within each, not all communities or species are discussed in detail. Rather, there is a greater focus on selected living resources where a better understanding of function and dynamics exists. Also, there is a greater emphasis on those species that serve as proxy for the health of overall community function.

The following information provides an assessment by sanctuary staff and subject area experts of the status and trends of living resources.

9. *What is the status of biodiversity and how is it changing?* Biodiversity is variation of life at all levels of biological organization, and also commonly encompasses diversity within a species (genetic diversity) and among species (species diversity), and comparative diversity among ecosystems (ecosystem diversity). While thorough historic or current inventories are not available to fully measure biodiversity and trends in the sanctuary, there are numerous species in the sanctuary that have experienced population declines in recent decades, which indicates compromised biodiversity in the system. Incremental improvement in our understanding of ecosystem processes and intensified regulatory oversight have led to anticipated reductions in some impacts, and some depleted marine mammal populations have increased in numbers. Nevertheless, the decline of seabird populations and limited information about deep-sea organisms support an undetermined overall trend for biodiversity.

The sanctuary's rocky intertidal community is biologically rich, with at least 300 documented species (Suchanek 1979, Dethier 1988), and new species are continuing to be discovered (deRivera et al. 2005). Long-term monitoring conducted by Olympic National Park in partnership with the sanctuary shows relatively stable trends in biodiversity (Dethier 1995, ONP unpublished data).

Less is known about the historic or current conditions of sub-tidal, open-water and deep-sea communities. A historical perspective suggests that many of the large mammals, high-order predators and keystone species no longer functioned in maintaining community structure when their stocks were depleted by commercial whaling, hunting and fishing (Roman and

Palumbi 2003, Springer et al. 2003, Alter et al. 2007), although this topic remains controversial (Trites et al. 2007, Wade et al. 2007). For example, the loss of sea otters in kelp forest ecosystems, like those in the sanctuary, can cause cascading trophic impacts to the kelp itself and significant changes in biodiversity of that habitat due to the loss of predation pressure on herbivorous invertebrates such as the sea urchin (Estes et al. 1989, Estes and Duggins 1995, Kvitek et al. 1998). More recently, harbor seal numbers were severely reduced during the first half of the 20th century in Washington state by a state-financed population control program (Jeffries et al. 2003). Harbor seal and sea otter populations have rebounded to the point where some people are concerned that the Marine Mammal Protection Act's effective removal of humans as predators on marine mammals is causing an imbalance in the system. Impacts of such dramatic population changes on trophic webs, although not well understood, are likely to have occurred, yet such impacts and recovery from them are difficult to estimate in the absence of historical information.

Although species richness (number of species in a community) may be relatively intact, as evidenced by few documented local vertebrate species extinctions, species evenness (the relative abundance of each species within a community) has undergone documented changes. Severe decreases in abundance of a species can impact ecosystem function. Changes in species evenness are exemplified by declining numbers of several locally breeding seabirds including the Common Murre, Tufted Puffin, Marbled Murrelet, Cassin's Auklet and Brandt's Cormorant. Populations of these species are considered declining in the area, and all are Washington state species of concern. The Marbled Murrelet is also federally threatened, and the Tufted Puffin is a federal species of concern. Four species of rockfish found in the sanctuary have been classified as overfished by the NOAA Fisheries Service (NMFS 2006). Nineteen fish species found within the sanctuary are identified as Washington state species of concern, of which eight also have some degree of federal protected status. Eleven marine mammals, three sea turtles and nine species of marine birds found in the sanctuary are on either federal or state species of concern lists across their range (Washington Department of Fish and Wildlife 2008). These are specific examples of the declining indices of biodiversity within the sanctuary.

Biodiversity within deepwater communities off the Washington coast is poorly understood, given the logistical challenges of conducting research in this habitat. Due to technological advances in undersea research, census and evaluation of ecological integrity of deep-sea habitats has only recently begun for fish assemblages (Rogers and Pikitch 1992, Jagielo et al. 2003) and coral and sponge communities (Etnoyer and Morgan 2003, Morgan et al. 2006, Brancato et al. 2007, Lumsden et al. 2007). There are indications that deepwater sponge and coral communities in the sanctuary have been impacted before many aspects of their basic biology and ecology could be ascertained (Brancato et al. 2007). Overall, there is much that is not known about the species richness and evenness of several important communities within the sanctuary. The importance of biodiversity of ocean ecosystems cannot be discounted when considering its central role in recovery of systems from perturbations (Worm et al. 2006).

10. *What is the status of environmentally sustainable fishing and how is it changing?* Environmentally sustainable fishing protects the fish and the environment in which they live while allowing responsible use of the species that come from that environment. It is designed to protect the integrity of ecosystem structure, productivity, function and biodiversity, including habitat and associated dependent and ecologically related biological communities.

The major commercial fisheries that operate in the sanctuary target groundfish (bottom trawl and longline), Pacific halibut, Dungeness crab, pink shrimp, sardines and salmon. In addition, there are significant recreational fisheries in the sanctuary that target salmon, groundfish and halibut. In general, professional fisheries managers appear optimistic that sustainable fisheries off the outer coast of Washington are possible under new management regimes following historical stock declines. Because this is the first condition report completed for the Olympic Coast sanctuary, and acknowledging the potentially long lag period between fishery actions and observable ecosystem level repercussions, this report examines this question from a long-term perspective, looking back one or more decades.

For several decades, commercial and recreational fisheries have extracted significant biomass from waters now encompassed by the sanctuary, in part using methods that are known to reduce complexity and damage living structures of seafloor habitats. Management actions, such as reduction of fish stocks to less than 50 percent of the unfished biomass, have the potential to alter ecosystems. Meanwhile, scientists are just beginning to understand fundamental elements of ecosystem function — the distribution and community composition of seafloor habitats, the distribution of and habitat requirements for different life stages of important commercial species, the significance of diverse age structures in sustaining fishery resources, and many other factors that influence community development and function. Recent fishery management measures implemented to reduce fishing effort, monitor and minimize bycatch, and reduce impacts to habitat appear to have assisted initial recovery of some overfished groundfish stocks and provide evidence for an improving trend.

The complexity of the groundfish stocks makes it difficult to make generalized statements about the sustainability of groundfish fisheries off the Washington coast. More than 90 species of groundfish, including over 60 species of rockfish, are managed under the Pacific Fisheries Management Council's (PFMC) Groundfish Fishery Management Plan. Beginning in the 1970s, improved understanding of life history characteristics led fisheries scientists to conclude that many of these species were incapable of sustaining high-intensity fishing pressure using modern fishing methods (PFMC 2008a). In recent years, West Coast groundfish stocks and fisheries have been in crisis, with steep declines in commercial ex-vessel value, overcapitalization, and several groundfish stocks depleted by a combination of fishing and natural factors (NMFS 2002). There are increasing concerns that our limited ability to forecast groundfish production from single species investigations is missing important natural and fishery-induced changes in the ecosystem and will not be able to forecast truly sustainable harvest policies (NMFS 2002).

Some groundfish species have been depleted in the past and have recovered quickly (e.g., English sole, Pacific whiting, and lingcod), while others are rebuilding more slowly (e.g., Pacific ocean perch) (PFMC 2008a). For depleted species, rebuilding programs are in place, with anticipated stock recovery period from several to over 80 years for different species. All species considered depleted are on track to be rebuilt by their respective schedules, which take into account their different life histories. Most groundfish populations are below 50 percent of their estimated unfished or original biomass (Figure 26). Of the 22 species of groundfish that occur in the sanctuary and are managed at the species level, 13 species have stocks that are considered healthy, three species are in a precautionary status, and five are depleted (canary, yelloweye, widow and darkblotched rockfish, and Pacific ocean perch) (PFMC 2008a). The remaining groundfish species are unassessed or managed in groupings or stock complexes, because individually they comprise a small part of the landed catch or stock assessments have not been completed. For some species, it is likely that insufficient information exists to develop adequate stock assessments.

Olympic Coast National Marine Sanctuary lies within the California Current marine ecosystem, which contains a complex web of pelagic and demersal fish resources, marine mammals, birds, invertebrate resources and elements of the food chain that support these more visible and economically valuable resources.

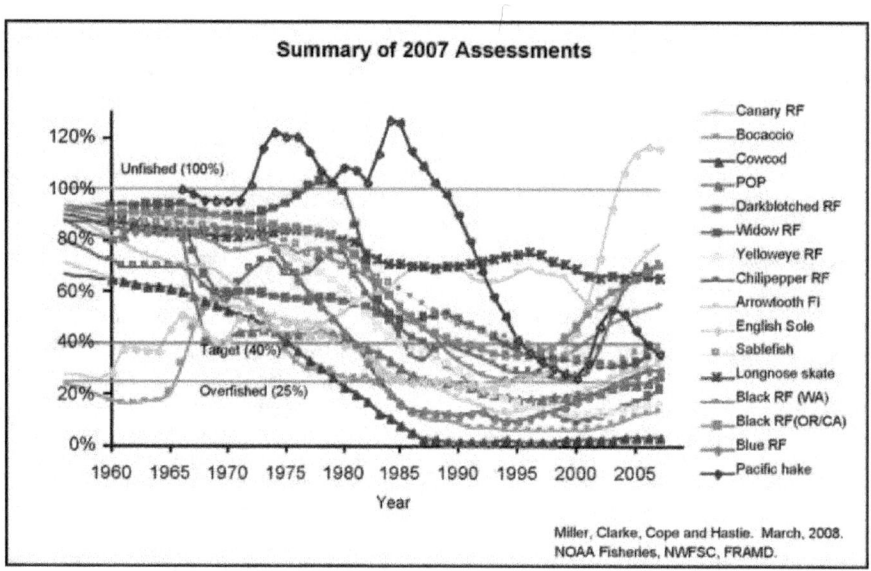

Figure 26. Historic trends in groundfish abundance off the West Coast.

This ecosystem undergoes significant climate fluctuations that last from a couple of years to several decades, and these cycles can both increase and mask the human impacts. For example, computer model simulations of the Northern California Current ecosystem (including the sanctuary) support the general assertion of a significant shift in the mid-1970s from a cold regime with high zooplankton productivity to a warmer regime with lower productivity and declining fish stocks (Field et al. 2001). There are some indications that the biomass off Washington of several rockfish species is high (per unit area) compared to Oregon and California, and this information has been taken into account for the management of some stocks (e.g., black rockfish). Survey data have been collected during NOAA Fisheries trawl surveys, but have not been quantitatively analyzed to determine if other groundfish stocks off Washington or in the sanctuary are more abundant than those off Oregon and California. Additional discussion of groundfish stocks is provided under Question 12.

Fisheries for crab and shrimp off the outer coast of Washington experience catch fluctuations but appear to be sustainable. The commercial Dungeness crab fishery has over 200 Washington coastal commercial Dungeness crab license holders. Dungeness crab landing data back to 1950 shows a large fluctuation in harvest, ranging from a low of 1,130 metric tons (2.5 million pounds) in 1981 to a high of 11,300 metric tons (25 million pounds) in 2004-2005, averaging 4,300 metric tons (9.5 million pounds) per year. This large fluctuation in landings is likely due to varying ocean conditions including water temperature,

food availability and ocean currents (http://wdfw.wa.gov/fish/shelfish/crabreg/comcrab/coast/index.htm). A fishery for pink shrimp off Washington peaked in 1988, with landings just over 18 million pounds and about 100 vessels involved. Within a few years, a dramatic decline in local abundance drove many fishers out of the fishery. Since 2000, the Washington coastal fishery has been stable, with landings of seven to eight million pounds annually and about 25 fishers participating. Management of the fishery is passive, with no stock assessment or mandatory logbook program in place. Most shrimp and crab fishing occurs off the central and southern coast of Washington (http://wdfw.wa.gov/fish/shelfish/shrimp/comm/index.html).

The Pacific halibut fishery is managed by the United States and Canada in a bilateral commission known as the International Pacific Halibut Commission. Annual catches and bycatch are strictly capped. Female halibut spawning biomass is estimated at three to four times above the historical minimum in the mid-1970s, indicating that the halibut population is in good condition (NMFS 2004).The commission refers to U.S. waters off the states of Washington, Oregon and California collectively as "Area 2A." Because populations in this area are considered healthy, catch limits in Area 2A for commercial, treaty and recreational halibut fishing are approximately double limits imposed in the early 1990s (http://www.iphc.washington.edu/halcom/default.htm).

Chinook and coho salmon are the main salmon species managed by PFMC off Washington's outer coast. In odd-numbered years, fisheries are also conducted near the Canadian border for pink salmon, which are primarily of Frasier River origin. Managing ocean salmon fisheries is an extremely complex task, due in large part to the wide oceanic distribution of the salmon and difficulty in estimating the size of salmon populations. Salmon numbers can vary widely from year to year, and returns can differ significantly from model estimates. In the past decade, landings from the ocean troll fishery off Washington (excluding the area south of Willapa Bay) varied five-fold for chinook and nine-fold for coho between low and high catch years, but no clear trends in landings are evident (PFMC 2008b). Salmon at all life history stages are affected by a wide variety of natural and human-caused factors in the ocean and on land, including ocean and climatic conditions, habitat degradation and loss, and predators (including humans). Other challenges to a sustainable salmon fishery off the Washington coast include judging the effects of different regional fisheries on salmon stocks, recovering salmon under the Endangered Species Act, dividing the harvest fairly, impacts from salmon aquaculture, competition between wild and hatchery salmon, and restoring freshwater habitat (PFMC 2008b).

The past decade has seen a paradigm shift in the management of fisheries from assessments of target stocks to a more holistic consideration of sustaining marine ecosystems, as well as fishing yields (NMFS 1999, Pikitch et al. 2004, Fluharty 2005, Tudela and Short 2005, Babcock et al. 2005). Fishery managers are now beginning to define and employ this practice (Zabel et al. 2003, Marasco et al. 2007, PSMFC 2005). The ecosystem-based fisheries management approach requires managers to consider all biotic interactions of predators, competitors and prey at all life history stages, the effects of physical factors such as climate and weather on fisheries biology and ecology, the complex interactions between fishes and their habitat, and the effects of fishing on fish stocks and their habitat (NMFS 1999).

Ecosystem-based fisheries management is designed to forge a healthy long-term relationship within and between ecosystems, economies, and societies (NMFS 1999, Gaichas 2008). Management of ecologically or environmentally sustainable fisheries includes consideration of measures such as the elimination of overfishing, minimizing habitat damage and loss, and insuring that the total of all biomass removed by all fisheries in an ecosystem does not exceed a total amount of system productivity (Pikitch et al. 2004). Such management goals also include maintaining populations of target species to conserve their natural role in maintaining ecosystem function while enabling sustainable reproduction rates, eliminating the use of fishing gear that creates a high level of bycatch or incidental contact with non-target species, and restricting removals from critical feeding, breeding and spawning grounds to protect marine ecosystems (NMFS 2006).

Fisheries management policies enacted on the West Coast and within the Olympic Coast sanctuary have been progressive steps to incorporate ecosystem-based fishery management concepts and improve trends toward restoring historical population levels. A variety of recent fishery management actions off the Washington coast, such as trawl footrope gear restrictions, low-rise nets that reduce bycatch, monitoring of bycatch, protection of Essential Fish Habitat (NMFS 2006), implementation of stock rebuilding plans, and establishment of temporary area closures (Rockfish Conservation Areas) to promote recovery of species under rebuilding plans, have provided early indications that depleted stocks can recover and these fisheries can be sustainably practiced.

*11. What is the status of non-indigenous species and how is it changing?* Relatively few exotic or non-indigenous species have been reported in the sanctuary and, of those, only a few are invasive and therefore threatening to community structure and function. Observations by coastal ecologists from Olympic National Park and the Olympic Coast sanctuary of increased amounts of the invasive brown algae *Sargassum muticum*, the documented range expansion of invasive ascidians (tunicates or sea squirts) (deRivera et al. 2005), and the encroachment of the invasive green crab to areas both south and north of the sanctuary all suggest that negative impacts from non-indigenous species are likely to increase in the future.

The sanctuary's rapid assessment intertidal surveys from 2001 and 2002 identified nine non-indigenous invertebrate species (two polychaetes, one amphipod, one bryozoan, four bivalves and one ascidian) and one algal species. A 2005 study of non-indigenous species along the West Coast in marine protected areas using settling plates located on buoys offshore found four non-indigenous species (one crustacean and three ascidians) inhabiting the Olympic Coast sanctuary (deRivera et al. 2005).

Ports and marinas tend to have higher numbers of invasive species due to transport by vessels (deRivera et al. 2005). There are no major ports located within sanctuary waters, and the few marinas that exist are relatively small, which may slow the number and severity of species invasions. However, shipping traffic through the sanctuary may provide a vector for non-indigenous species via transport on hulls and discharge of ballast water. To minimize this risk, Washington state recently strengthened regulations covering ballast water exchange. Ships traveling from outside the U.S. Exclusive Economic Zone must exchange ballast water no closer than 200 nautical miles (374 kilometers) offshore, while ships considered U.S. coastal traffic, including Canadian waters, must exchange ballast water no closer than 50 nautical miles (93 kilometers) offshore (http://groups.ucanr.org/Ballast_Outreach/

Laws_and_Regulations/Washington_State.htm). Even with regulations in place, there is a need for basic understanding of the spatial and temporal patterns of invasions (deRivera et al. 2005).

**12. *What is the status of key species and how is it changing?*** Key species (e.g., keystone species, indicator species, sensitive species and those targeted for special protection) within the sanctuary are numerous, and all cannot be covered here. Emphasis is placed on examples from various primary habitats of the sanctuary: seabirds for nearshore and pelagic habitats, sea otters for nearshore habitat, and rockfish for deep seabed habitats. In this response, status refers primarily to population numbers, as opposed to condition or health of the populations as addressed under Question 13. Several species of seabirds that breed and feed in the sanctuary, several species of cetaceans that forage in or visit sanctuary waters, and a few groundfish species that inhabit the sanctuary are reduced in numbers in comparison to historical levels. In many cases, their recovery is uncertain and linked to dynamic and poorly understood ecosystem-level processes.

Seabirds are relatively numerous, conspicuous, and forage across multiple habitat types and trophic levels. For these reasons, they are often considered indicators of ocean conditions, and the status of their populations provide insight into ecosystem health (Parrish and Zador 2003, Piatt et al. 2007). Many feed on forage fish, a critical link in the food chain, but one that is difficult to quantify by direct observation. Five species of marine birds that breed in the sanctuary are on federal or state species of concern lists: Common Murre, Marbled Murrelet, Tufted Puffin, Cassin's Auklet, and Brandt's Cormorant. Trends and common concerns among these seabirds are long-term declines in their population sizes (Wahl and Tweit 2000, Wahl et al. 2005, Raphael 2006); vulnerability to human disturbances such as oil spills, habitat disruption and fisheries bycatch (Piatt et al. 2002, Raphael 2006); and susceptibility to natural disturbances such as ENSO events (Graybill and Hodder 1985, Wilson 1991, Piatt et al. 2002, Wahl et al. 2005). Some population levels do appear to be stabilizing at values lower than historical levels; however, a longer time series is needed to determine a trend (Lance et al. 2008).

A closer examination of the Common Murre population provides insight into some factors affecting the status of all seabirds on the Washington coast. The murre population declined dramatically in 1982 and 1983, coinciding with a severe El Niño-Southern Oscillation (ENSO), and has not recovered to pre-1983 levels since that time (Warheit and Thompson 2003). Aside from other ENSO events, it has been suggested that the population has not recovered due to a combination of oil spills, disturbance at breeding colonies (e.g., historic Naval bombing practices),

and gillnet mortality (Warheit and Thompson 2003). Two oil spill events have occurred in recent times on the Washington coast, one in 1988 (the Nestucca) and the other 1991 (the Tenyo Maru). In both spills, Common Murres were a significant proportion of the bird mortality (74 percent and 73 percent respectively of the birds recovered; Parrish personal communication). There were 9,275 Common Murre mortalities documented from the Nestucca spill (Parrish personal communication), from which total mortality was estimated at 30,000 murres off the outer coast of Washington (Manuwal et al. 2001). During the Tenyo Maru oil spill, 3,157 Common Murre mortalities were documented, suggesting that a potentially sizable proportion of the total Washington state Common Murre population may have been killed by the spill (The Tenyo Maru Oil Spill Natural Resource Trustees 2000). Although the sanctuary's Common Murre population showed signs of recovery through the 1990s, the number of birds has diminished greatly relative to pre-spill numbers, and modest declines have been found in recent years (Manuwal et al. 2001). At the breeding colony on Tatoosh Island, Common Murre populations have also been affected by an influx of avian predators, including Bald Eagles, Peregrine Falcons and nest-depredating Glaucous-winged Gulls (Parrish et al. 2001). The multiple stressors affecting the sluggish recovery of Common Murres may be indicative of the challenges facing the long-term recovery of other seabirds.

The sea otter is often considered a keystone species because of the strong top-down influence they have on the nearshore kelp ecosystem. Sea otters are of high interest because sea otters were extirpated from Washington state by commercial pelt hunters by 1911, then were reintroduced in 1969 and 1970 (Lance et al. 2004). This population has been counted annually since 1989 and has shown increases the past few years, with a peak of 1,121 animals in 2008 (Jameson and Jeffries 2008). However, the sea otter population remains vulnerable to catastrophic events (e.g., oil spills), and the population rate of increase has been slower than expected. The population is still considered to be below the estimated carrying capacity based on historical and regional habitat use, which includes rocky, sandy and mixed substrates (Laidre et al. 2002; Lance et al. 2004). However, habitat loss in estuaries such as Grays Harbor could reduce the actual carrying capacity, and it remains to be seen if the projected rocky habitat density (7.1 otters per kilometer of shoreline) will be attained along the Olympic shoreline. The sea otter remains a federal species of concern and an endangered species within Washington state. The sea otter population remains vulnerable because of its small size, limited genetic diversity, existing exposure to pathogens, and risks from spills (see Question 13).

Indicator species of the deep-sea environs are not clearly defined due to limited information about this remote region of the ocean. Very little is known about the status of deep-sea coral and sponge communities (Brancato et al. 2007, Whitmire and Clarke 2007). Rockfish assemblages are a key vertebrate guild that could serve as a proxy for the condition of deep-sea communities. Unfortunately, the status of discrete fish stocks relevant to Washington state is not well defined for most rockfish species independently from the West Coast assessment effort. In general, the PFMC has indicated its support for regional management of stocks where appropriate and when there are data to support such a management structure. Stock assessment authors are asked to review and evaluate all available data to determine whether a regional management approach would be recommended for the stock being assessed. In some cases, however, even when adequate data are available to support more discrete management, the PFMC has chosen to continue to manage those stocks on a coast-wide basis. Groundfish fisheries are also discussed under Question 10.

13. *What is the condition or health of key species and how is it changing?* As indicated above in Question 12, the sanctuary selected certain seabirds, sea otters and rockfish as key species or indicators of ecosystem health. The condition or health of each is discussed below. Exposure to pathogens that have killed sea otters in California, bioaccumulation of organic pollutants in high-order predators, modification of natural population structure through harvest, and uncertainty about altered oceanographic conditions associated with climate change all contribute to degradation of ecosystem integrity. Long-term implications of these conditions are uncertain.

Most wildlife populations in the sanctuary are relatively healthy and unburdened by contaminants, pathogens or related maladies. There are, however, notable exceptions. The sea otter population has been shown to carry several potentially lethal pathogens. In a study where tissue samples were collected from 30 live sea otters, 80 percent of the otters tested positive for the distemper viral complex *Morbillivirus* and 60 percent tested positive for the protozoan *Toxoplasma gondii* (Brancato et al. 2006). No direct negative health effects in the Washington population have yet been documented from these pathogens; however, Toxoplasma has been a cause of mortality in California sea otters (Miller et al. 2004). In addition, there was a positive correlation between chemical contaminants such as PCBs and pathogen levels, with the latter used as a proxy for immunosuppression (Brancato et al. 2006). Furthermore, PCB levels were correlated with a significant reduction of vitamin A stores in the liver, yet overall, tissue concentrations of assayed contaminants were relatively low in Washington sea otters (Brancato et al. 2006). Fat-soluble contaminants are generally considered to bioaccumulate or increase in concentration when moving up the food web (Cockcroft et al. 1989). Top predators in the region, such as killer whales, have been shown to carry high contaminant loads (e.g., PCBs and PBDEs) in their blubber (Ross et al. 2000, Ross 2006), though the population effects of such high contaminant loads are unknown.

Sea otter populations were regionally extirpated in the early 1900s, but 59 individuals were reintroduced to the area in 1969 and 1970. Consequently, there is reduced genetic variation in the Washington coast sea otter population when compared with ancient sea otter remains, as determined by analysis of DNA sequences (Larson et al. 2002). Reduced genetic variability is generally considered to impart deleterious effects such as reduced fecundity, higher juvenile mortality and reduced capacity to combat environmental stressors (Ralls et al. 1983, Lance et al. 2004). Sea otter populations should be closely monitored for such adverse effects, and to determine when the population crosses the strait, potentially breeding with the population around Vancouver Island, which could increase genetic variability. At the moment, the condition or health of sea otters is stable, but merits watching.

Age structure, an important measure of population integrity, has been affected by extractive activities. Some rockfish populations have been shown to have reduced numbers of larger, older fish, a factor that could affect their recovery rate (PFMC 2008a). There is a positive relationship between fecundity and age in long-lived Pacific rockfish such as the genus *Sebastes* (Eldridge and Jarvis 1995). Furthermore, larvae of larger, older rockfish are better conditioned in terms of higher growth rates and ability to withstand starvation (Berkeley et al. 2004). Removals of older individuals from long-lived species can also have broader ecological impacts (Heppell et al. 2005). However, in most cases, the status of the larger, older fish within the population is unknown (i.e., it has not been determined whether the older fish are simply missing because they have been removed from the population, or are not available to the data source — e.g., the fishery or survey used as the index of abundance in the assessment).

Age structure and mortality rates are also in question in some bird populations on the coast. Common Murres on Tatoosh Island have experienced documented breeding failures during recent years, partially attributed to oil spills and observed heavy predation by raptors and gulls, but also possibly due to low food supply during critical breeding periods (Parrish et al. 2001, Warheit and Thompson 2003). Because they are long-lived, an occasional year of poor productivity may not impact the population significantly, but multiple years or successive years of breeding failure would likely have future impacts on the population. Baseline mortality rates for Common Murres and other seabirds are currently being examined through the Coastal Observation and Seabird Survey Team program, a comprehensive coast-wide program initiated in 1999 to document beach-cast bird trends over time (Hass and Parrish 2000). Recent demographic studies of Marbled Murrelets in the region have indicated that they have had low nesting success in recent years (Raphael and Bloxton 2008), which may inhibit their recovery or at least slow the rate of recovery.

14. *What are the levels of human activities that may influence living resource quality and how are they changing?* Fishing has in the past and continues today to affect sanctuary habitats and biota in a number of ways. For several decades, bottom-contact fishing gear used by commercial fishers damaged seafloor habitat widely in the sanctuary and altered benthic communities by removing biogenic structures and disturbing infauna. As discussed above, recent fishery management actions have significantly reduced, but not completely eliminated, the potential for further habitat damage. However, because the distribution of deep-sea coral and sponge communities has never been quantified or sufficiently mapped within the sanctuary, it is difficult to determine the extent of overlap between existing biogenic communities and current fishing activity. From the ecosystem perspective, there remain concerns that industrial fishing targets larger, older fish, which alters age structure and can reduce the breeding potential of long-lived species such as certain rockfish species (NRC 2006). Moreover, past overfishing has caused dramatic reduction in some fish stocks (see Figure 26). Recent closure of large portions of the sanctuary to fishing techniques that target species most vulnerable to overfishing is expected to mitigate past impacts to both seafloor habitats and ecosystem integrity, and indicates the potential for recovery.

Oil spills remain the most serious threat to local populations of marine organisms. Although no major spills have occurred within the sanctuary since the Tenyo Maru spill in 1991, some populations, such as the Common Murre, have not yet recovered from that spill. The establishment of the Area To Be Avoided has helped to keep oil barges, tankers and other large commercial vessels away from the most biologically sensitive areas, and the rescue tug stationed at Neah Bay has averted several hazardous situations. However, because of the heavy shipping traffic using the Strait of Juan de Fuca, combined with the challenging seas of the eastern North Pacific, the sanctuary still remains at risk from a catastrophic spill.

## Maritime Archaeological Resources Status and Trends

Olympic Coast National Marine Sanctuary has a rich maritime heritage where lives, languages, communities and cultures are constantly shaped by the sea. The Makah, Quileute, Hoh and Quinault peoples traditionally lived at the water's edge, thriving on the riches of the ocean — plants, fish, shellfish, seabirds and marine

mammals. The waters of the sanctuary were highways that linked native peoples all along the coast as they traveled by canoe while mastering currents, weather and tides. The rugged Olympic Coast can also be treacherous, especially during winter storms when high winds and strong currents can push ships dangerously close to the rocky islands, reefs and shoreline — over 180 ships were wrecked or lost at sea in or near sanctuary waters in the years from 1808 to 1972 (Figure 27). The following discussion addresses issues facing these sanctuary resources with respect to their integrity and condition, potential hazards they pose, and ways in which human activities may impact their integrity.

The following information provides an assessment by sanctuary staff and subject area experts of the status and trends pertaining to the current state of the sanctuary's maritime archaeological resources.

## Maritime Archaeological Resources Status & Trends

| # | Issue | Rating | Basis for Judgment | Description of Findings |
|---|-------|--------|--------------------|--------------------------|
| 15 | Integrity | ? | Deepwater wrecks stable; shallow wrecks subject to environmental degradation; lack of monitoring to determine trend. | The diminished condition of selected archaeological resources has reduced, to some extent, their historical, scientific or educational value, and may affect the eligibility of some sites for listing in the National Register of Historic Places. |
| 16 | Threat to Environment | — | Historic wrecks did not carry substantial quantities of hazardous cargoes. | Known maritime archaeological resources pose few or no environmental threats. |
| 17 | Human Activities | ? | Unauthorized salvaging nearshore; fishing activities and cable installations offshore. | Selected activities have resulted in measurable impacts to maritime archaeological resources, but evidence suggests effects are localized, not widespread. |

Status: Good   Good/Fair   Fair   Fair/Poor   Poor   Undet.

Trends: Improving (▲), Not Changing (—), Getting Worse (▼), Undetermined Trend (?), Question not applicable (N/A)

15. *What is the integrity of maritime archaeological resources and how is it changing?* In general, the sanctuary's maritime archaeological resources are not being managed in accordance with the National Historic Preservation Act (NHPA) due to limited funding, and efforts to locate and assess maritime archaeological resources have been extremely limited.

While the Olympic Coast has been the focus of human communities for thousands of years and has figured prominently in Pacific Northwest maritime history, there is no agency-sponsored inventory of submerged maritime archaeological resources in the offshore environment in the sanctuary. The sanctuary's inventory contains information of approximately 180 known vessel losses, and limited efforts to locate specific wrecks have revealed only a few wreck sites..

Due to limited survey effort, few deepwater shipwrecks are known. Of these, only the World War II submarine USS *Bugara* has received any survey attention. Archaeological resources in deep offshore waters are generally in a more stable environment because such environments tend to be calmer and have fewer physical and biological processes accelerating ship degradation compared to nearshore sites. Historical and recent bottom trawling is one probable impact to offshore maritime archaeological resources that has potentially damaged submerged historic resources. Because the majority of wreck locations are unknown, the impacts from historical and recent trawling are unknown. Anecdotal reports have indicated damage from fishing gear or fishing practices, such as entanglement and snagging. The development of underwater technologies now affords the public the opportunity to locate and visit deepwater archaeological resources in the offshore environment. As with divers visiting accessible nearshore archaeological sites, the diving community must be educated on the regulations in place in order to protect these non-renewable resources. In the absence of a robust cultural resources education program, the maritime resources may be subject to vandalism, looting or damage.

Shallow shipwrecks are subject to severe environmental degradation resulting from natural processes such as ocean surge, north Pacific storms, strong currents and sea level rise (Figure 28). The *General Meigs* and the *Austria* are two wrecks that are heavily impacted from natural destruction. However, no monitoring of changing conditions is currently being conducted.

There have already been significant studies of both the late prehistoric and older archaeological sites, but much remains to be learned. To date, most of the efforts have focused upon the more recent sites, but knowledge of the sites associated with mid-Holocene shorelines is relatively limited. Although some collaborative monitoring of prehistoric sites is currently being conducted by Olympic National Park, the sanctuary and Makah Tribal Historic Preservation Officers, it is minimal and informal. However, data from other parts of the northwest coast suggest that there may be several different types of prehistoric archaeological resources in the sanctuary. Features such as late prehistoric fish traps and canoe runs are known to be present near the sanctuary, and examples of both may be present within it. There is also the possibility that ancient archaeological sites could be

Figure 27. Olympic Coast National Marine Sanctuary is the graveyard for many shipwrecks. Human error, treacherous weather, dangerous reefs and headlands and ships' navigational or operational failures still contribute to this place's hazardous reputation among mariners. This anchor is nearly all that remains of the bark *Austria*, grounded at Cape Alava in 1887.

Figure 28. Wreck of the *Lamut*, a Russian merchant ship lost in 1943 near Quillayute Needles.

present on inundated late Pleistocene and early Holocene shorelines in the sanctuary. Given the absence of direct evidence, it is not possible to address the conditions of such resources (if they are present). Data from other parts of the northwest coast suggest that such resources are likely to be relatively durable; however, like shipwrecks, prehistoric archaeological resources could be adversely affected by wave energy (particularly those resources in the intertidal zone and shorelines), commercial fishing activities and recreational divers. Prehistoric archaeological sites in the intertidal zone and shorelines are also subject to looting and other human disturbance, but little monitoring, education or enforcement takes place.

There is considerable variation in the integrity of the known archaeological resources near the sanctuary. Nearly all of the late prehistoric sites associated with the modern shoreline are actively eroding. Data exist that document the loss of cultural deposits due to shoreline erosion, and it can be anticipated that rising sea levels will accelerate the rate of this loss. Significant loss of cultural deposits has also been caused by development in and around modern shoreline communities. As can be expected, development is less of a factor in the Olympic National Park. Although relatively limited, some additional damage to cultural deposits along the modern shoreline has occurred due to vandalism. While knowledge of the integrity of the older mid-Holocene sites is more limited, these sites are mostly located in nearshore forest settings and are not being impacted by shoreline erosion. Historic impacts on these sites have resulted primarily from activities such as logging and the construction of logging roads. Given that these sites tend to be located in relatively remote places and are difficult to detect, there are no known cases of damage due to vandalism.

*16. Do maritime archaeological resources pose an environmental hazard and how is this threat changing?* The sanctuary's inventory of known maritime archaeological resources suggests that the potential for shipwrecks in the sanctuary to pose an environmental hazard to sanctuary resources is minimal. Therefore, the situation is considered to be good and not changing.

The historic shipwrecks (at least 50 years old) in the sanctuary include both merchant and military vessels that sank during wartime, as well as older peacetime sinkings and groundings. However, for the purposes of wreck removal, salvage, and pollution response, most of the vessels in question would be from post-1910, when naval and commercial vessels began to shift from coal to oil bunkers (Dahl 2001). It is likely that earlier wrecks are no longer intact and did not carry substantial quantities of hazardous cargoes or fuel oil.

Given the above criteria that constitute "historic wrecks" with potential to pose an environmental hazard, the sanctuary has 12 known vessels in this category (OCNMS Shipwreck Database).

Of these 12 vessels, only one, the General Miegs, has been identified as a source of oil leakage into the environment (Clark et al. 1975). However, no monitoring is currently taking place. There are occasional reports of mystery spills (oil sheen reported on the water from an unknown source). This can indicate a release from a wreck; however, this does not occur frequently or consistently enough to give a strong indication of a release from a submerged wreck. It is more likely that this is the result of an illegal discharge of oily ballast or other accidental and unreported release from a vessel (Helton 2003).

*17. What are the levels of human activities that may influence maritime archaeological resource quality and how are they changing?* Human activities in the sanctuary have impacted maritime archaeological resources, but a general lack of assessment makes the trend undetermined. This is based on unauthorized salvaging that is taking place in the intertidal zone of the sanctuary and fishing activities and cable installations that are occurring in the offshore zone of the sanctuary.

Prehistoric sites in the intertidal zone and shorelines are subject to erosion, and wave action and storm events uncover new materials every year. As resources are unearthed, they are subject to the threat of looting and vandalism. There is little monitoring, enforcement and education taking place to offset this threat.

Historical and recent bottom trawling can potentially impact maritime archaeological resources in the offshore zone of the sanctuary. Incidental damage to resources may occur through impacts from bottom-contact fishing gear (trawl, longlines, etc.), anchoring and derelict fishing gear. However, because the majority of wreck locations are unknown, the impacts from historical and recent trawling are unknown. Recent closures of large areas of the sanctuary to bottom trawling will reduce these threats. The creation of new or larger areas restricting bottom-contact gear may indirectly protect historical resources.

Also threatening resources in the offshore zone is the trenching of submerged communication cables. As has been mentioned, the installation of underwater cables can negatively impact benthic habitat in the immediate vicinity of the cable, but the impacts are localized to within a few meters to either side of the cable route. In advance of cable installations, route surveys are conducted to identify and avoid maritime archaeological resources, yet there is potential for buried remains to be undetected by surveys and subsequently damaged by cable trenching equipment.

Other human activities affecting archaeological resources in the sanctuary include:

■ With more sophisticated diving technology becoming available (rebreathers, affordable side-scan sonar, etc.) and the allure of treasure or artifacts, some treasure hunters are moving to deeper waters. Any vessel or site could be considered in danger of damage from scavenging or vandalism, but those known in local histories as carrying valuables, such as the steamer Pacific, should be located and evaluated soon. The threat of looting or vandalism increases as erosion and human use and access rates increase.

■ Human use disturbance due to management activities (placement of privies in the wilderness) or lack of mitigating measures (use of informal social trails or campsites) can potentially impact land-based sites that were once coastal. This threat is decreasing due to improved interagency consultation.

■ Mineral extraction activities: Intertidal maritime cultural resources could be imperiled by beach mining activities (gravel, sand, gold, etc.) as have been proposed in the past. Significant timber cutting or inland mining has the potential to increase erosion to river and stream mouths, altering or imperiling intertidal and nearshore resources.

■ The possibility of installation of offshore power generation or aquaculture facilities.

There is a lack of assessment, monitoring and enforcement for maritime archaeological resources in the sanctuary. However, the situation for archaeological resources on lands immediately adjacent to the sanctuary is somewhat better understood. Sites in these areas are relatively more accessible; therefore, monitoring is accomplished with more ease. These sites represent a variety of different conditions and are influenced by varying combinations of both natural processes and human activities. As such, some are much more threatened than others. The human activities threatening archaeological sites near the sanctuary are mostly related to development and terrestrial resource extraction (principally logging). Presumably, both types of activities will continue in nearshore areas for the foreseeable future. Shoreline erosion is also a serious threat to the survival of many archaeological sites, and this effect will become more severe if sea level rise continues to occur in the coming decades (Pendleton et al. 2004).

# Response to Pressures

The Office of National Marine Sanctuaries has a mandate to maintain biological communities and protect and restore native habitats, populations and ecological processes within its boundaries, while allowing compatible uses. A sanctuary management plan establishes research, monitoring and resource protection priorities and programs to address key threats or pressures. In addition to guidance provided through the management plan, sanctuary regulations specific to each site establish a range of activities that are prohibited or are authorized through a sanctuary permit if it can be demonstrated that the activity supports a sanctuary management objective and it will not substantially injure sanctuary resources. Olympic Coast sanctuary staff have worked with others in the sanctuary system to review concerns and develop consistent policies associated with activities common to multiple sanctuaries, such as submarine cable installation, alternative energy development, and anchoring of research buoys.

In addition to sanctuary authorities, other federal, state and tribal authorities, regulations and policies govern the conduct of specific activities within the sanctuary. The nature of overlapping jurisdictions and authorities requires coordination and collaboration between resource managers to achieve marine conservation objectives. The sanctuary superintendent must balance the diverse interests of citizens, organizations and partner agencies and make informed decisions that protect resources without inappropriately constraining sanctuary users and stakeholders. To better understand those interests and enlist help from those we serve, the sanctuary superintendent meets regularly with an Advisory Council that is comprised of representatives of Indian tribes, state and local governments, other federal agencies, industry, conservation organizations, and citizens. In 2007, the coastal treaty Indian tribes, the state of Washington and the sanctuary established an Intergovernmental Policy Council to provide a forum for the tribal, state and federal governments to coordinate activities within the sanctuary.

This section describes current responses and research and resource protection initiatives addressing selected pressures. Current responses are based on implementation of the 1994 sanctuary management plan and regulations, as well as specific programs to address threats which have emerged since the 1994 management plan. Strategies to address prioritized threats or pressures will be further evaluated and adapted during the management plan review process, scheduled to begin in September 2008.

## Water Quality
### *Water Quality Monitoring*

The sanctuary strives to understand, maintain and improve water quality within the sanctuary (Figure 29), and regulations prohibit discharges into sanctuary waters. Since 2000, nearshore oceanographic moorings have been deployed to measure water temperature and, as funding has allowed, the program has been expanded to cover a greater area and include additional sensors to measure salinity, dissolved oxygen, currents, plankton density and other standard environmental parameters (Figure 30). Information from these moorings, as well as data collected from periodic surveys from NOAA vessels, will lead to a better understanding of the links between the physical, chemical, and biological processes in productive nearshore waters and the connections with offshore and deeper waters. In turn, these data are useful to federal, tribal, university and state-sponsored studies of harmful algal blooms, helping to assess potential threats to human health and the health of birds and other marine mammals. These data are also used to correlate with intertidal invertebrate and algae studies, assist in oil spill response and improve our understanding of hypoxic conditions that have been measured off the Washington and Oregon coasts in recent years. In an effort to establish baseline levels of persistent organic pollutants (industrial contaminants that remain for decades and can accumulate in organisms) in the ecosystem, the sanctuary has led and collaborated on several projects to measure contaminant levels in sediments, invertebrates and sea otters, against which future data can be compared.

Figure 29. Water quality data is collected by lowering equipment into the ocean to sample a water column profile from the bottom to the surface. This rosette is a series of instruments on a metal frame that measures temperature, pressure, salinity, oxygen content, algae content and other factors, and features chambers to collect water samples at predetermined depths.

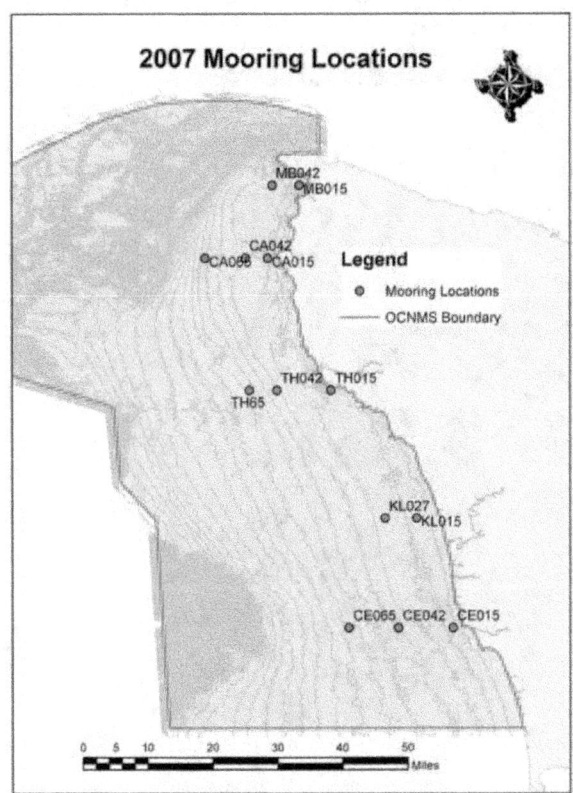

**2007 Mooring Locations**

MB042
MB015

CA042
CA065 CA015

**Legend**

○ Mooring Locations
— OCNMS Boundary

TH042 TH015
TH65

KL027
KL015

CE065 CE042 CE015

0 5 10 20 30 40 50
Miles

Figure 30. Remote sensors on fixed moorings collect information on physical and biological properties of sanctuary waters at 13 locations that were selected to capture variability in nearshore ocean processes. Source: OCNMS

### Vessel Discharges

Sewage and graywater discharges from large vessels (300 gross registered tons or more), including cruise ships and container ships, are a concern in state and sanctuary waters. In 2004, a Memorandum of Understanding between Washington state, the Port of Seattle, and the cruise ship industry included an agreement to avoid dumping of biosolids (sewage sludge or solids from wastewater treatment systems) within 12 nautical miles (22 kilometers) of shore. In 2007, this agreement was expanded to avoid such discharge in all sanctuary waters. According to Port of Seattle statistics, approximately 150 cruise ship trips between Seattle and Alaska occurred in 2007, and each week-long trip generated about 106,000 liters (28,000 gallons) of sewage sludge. Cruise ships transiting the sanctuary are currently not prohibited from discharging minimally treated sewage, graywater and blackwater, in accordance with state and federal law. Consequently, the rapidly expanding cruise ship industry in the Pacific Northwest may have growing potential to impact sanctuary waters if not properly managed.

### Area To Be Avoided Monitoring and Compliance

A catastrophic discharge of oil from a maritime accident poses the single greatest risk to the sanctuary. Olympic Coast sanctuary staff worked with the U.S. Coast Guard and the International Maritime Organization to establish an Area To Be Avoided as a buffer and provide greater response time for assistance to foundering vessels along this rocky and environmentally sensitive coast (Figure 31). All ships transiting the area and carrying cargoes of oil or hazardous materials and all ships 1,600 gross tons and larger are requested to avoid this area. In addition, sanctuary staff participated in multi-party discussions that led to modifications to the vessel traffic lanes at the western entrance to the Strait of Juan de Fuca in an effort to increase the safety of commercial vessel transits through this busy area.

Since 1998, the sanctuary has been obtaining monthly vessel position files from the Canadian Coast Guard's radar site on Vancouver Island (Galasso 2000). This information is displayed as tracklines on a geographic information system. The data also includes vessel attributes that allow spatial and temporal analysis of behavior and trends, based on vessel characteristics. The Marine Exchange of Seattle has also been providing the sanctuary with data from the Automated Identification System to augment vessel transit monitoring. The sanctuary uses this information to create monthly transit plots of non-complying vessels, which are used as part of an outreach effort to the marine industry. Letters are sent out under signature of the sanctuary superintendent and the Coast Guard Captain of the Port to non-complying vessels observed within the Area To Be Avoided. The response by the maritime industry has been very favorable, with an approximated compliance rate of 98.8 percent in 2007.

### Oil Spill Prevention

The sanctuary works closely with the U.S. Coast Guard, Washington Department of Ecology, Makah Office of Marine Safety and other organizations on oil spill response and preparedness by participating in oil spill drills, supporting a rescue tug stationed in Neah Bay, participating in discussions of alternative response technologies, prioritizing allocation of oil spill restoration funds, and reviewing proposed legislation, regulations and documentation. Since 1999, Washington state has funded a seasonal rescue tug stationed at Neah Bay to quickly respond to vessels that may need assistance. As of February 2008, the tug has escorted, stood by or assisted 40 ships that were disabled or had reduced maneuvering or propulsion capability while fishing or transporting oil and other cargo through the sanctuary and along the Strait of Juan de Fuca.

The sanctuary also has developed a site-specific Sanctuaries Hazardous Incident Emergency Logistics Database System (SHIELDS), which is designed to aid in spill response by providing a comprehensive reference and resource data tool.

## Habitat
### Habitat Mapping

The sanctuary does not directly manage fisheries within sanctuary waters; however, sanctuary research informs fisheries management entities, particularly on habitats within sanctuary boundaries. Starting in 2000, the sanctuary embarked on a project to characterize seafloor habitats within the sanctuary, using advanced acoustic and optical technologies to create digital images, and verifying those images using remotely operated vehicles and drop-cameras (Figure 32). The imagery helps to characterize the types, distribution and abundance of seafloor habitats, and groundtruthing helps to verify classification results, as well as to provide new habitat information. Furthering this research was a key recommendation of Washington's Ocean Action Plan (Office of the Governor 2006) and is a priority for the Intergovernmental Policy Council. These efforts can support crucial management issues, such as protecting critical habitats, identifying areas of undisturbed deep-sea coral and sponge communities, or examining fishing regulations to aid in the recovery of declining fish populations.

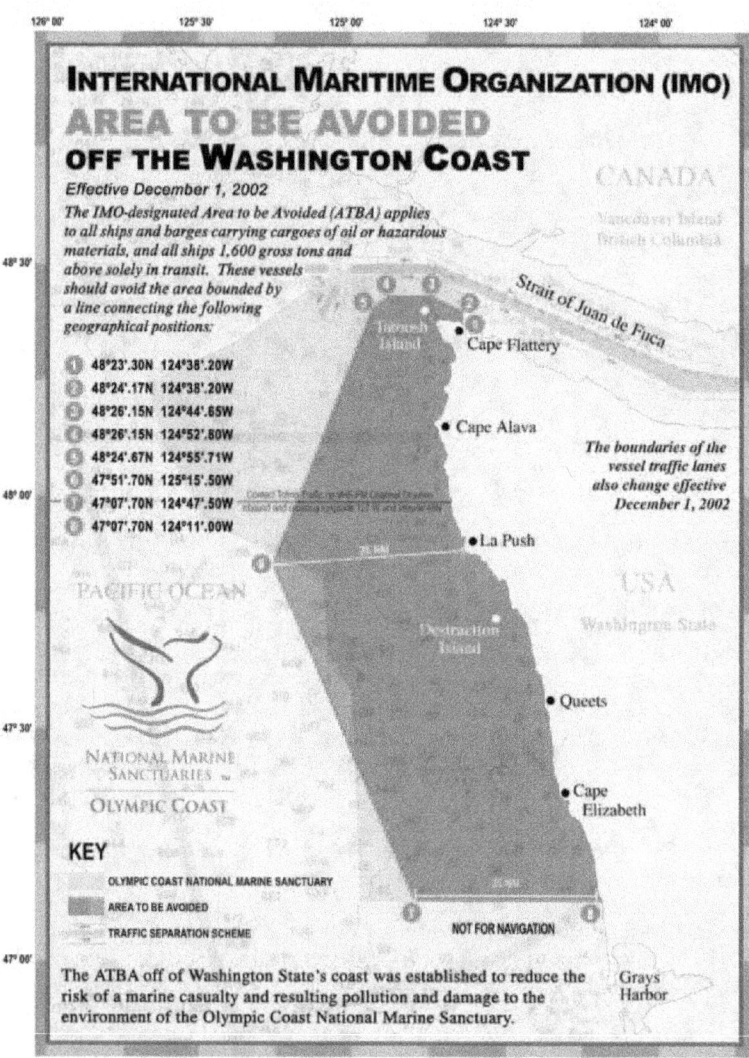

Figure 31. Map of Olympic Coast National Marine Sanctuary (in blue) and the Area To Be Avoided (in red). Flyer: OCNMS

### Deep Sea Coral
### Research and Conservation

In 2004 and 2006, sanctuary staff, in partnership with the National Centers of Coastal Ocean Science conducted side-scan and video surveys of offshore habitats. The focus of this initiative was to document the presence of hard-bottom habitats in deepwater areas of the sanctuary and video survey any associated living communities. Hard substrates often harbor diverse assemblages of invertebrates and fish, including corals, sponges and other extremely slow-growing fauna that are particularly sensitive to human disturbances. Several species of corals and sponges were documented at 14 of the 15 sites surveyed in 2006; sites located both inside and outside of the protective Essential Fish Habitat conservation area (Olympic 2). Numerous gorgonians, two stony coral species (*Lophelia pertusa* and *Desmophyllum dianthus*) and small patches of the reef-building sponge (*Farrea occa*) were found (Figure 33). Some anthropogenic disturbance to these seafloor communities was also documented. Future explorations will continue to improve our understanding of deep coral and sponge habitat, its distribution and ecosystem functions, and potential pressures on that system (Brancato et al. 2007). http://sanctuaries.noaa.gov/science/conservation/bowlby.html

### Derelict Fishing Gear and Marine Debris

In 2005, the sanctuary was awarded funds from NOAA's Marine Debris Program for a pilot project to identify and remove derelict fishing gear in the northern part of the sanctuary, as well as to develop safe operating protocols for gear removal operations while working in the open ocean environment. This pilot project was a partnership with the Makah Tribe with a goal to build capacity in an affected community to conduct future derelict gear removal projects. Fishery managers and fishermen were interviewed and multiple target areas over a few kilometers of nearshore waters near Cape Flattery were surveyed by sonar and divers. Three abandoned fishing nets and several crab pots were located and recovered, along with evidence of ghost fishing (Figure 34). The extent of the problem over many kilometers of the outer coast and deeper waters of the sanctuary remains unclear.

Another grant the sanctuary received from NOAA's Marine Debris program in 2007 supported collaborative development of a long-term strategy to remove accumulated marine debris from the outer coast of Washington state, beaches adjacent to the sanctuary and beyond. State and federal agency representatives joined with Native American tribes and non-government organizations to outline a strategy that addresses both the remote wilderness shores of Olympic National Park and tribal reservations and the more accessible areas where beach driving facilitates removal of marine debris. Partner agencies formed a new organization, Washington Clean Coast Alliance, to coordinate public outreach, volunteer coordination, and event planning, as a successor to the private citizen who was largely responsible for cleanup efforts dating back to 2000. The alliance's first event in April 2008, scheduled to coincide with Earth Day, was a great success. More than 1,100 volunteers joined the effort and enjoyed the beach while removing nearly 23 tons of debris.

### Fiber-Optic Cable Permit Compliance and Monitoring

In 2006, the Pacific Crossing responded to sanctuary and tribal concerns over improper burial of the Pacific Crossing PC-1 fiber-optic submarine telecommunication cables by reinstalling the cable through the sanctuary. The goal of this effort was to minimize risks of interactions with fishing gear, reduce cable damage, and to minimize ongoing impacts to seafloor habitats. Sanctuary regulations generally prohibit seafloor disturbances. Post-installation assessment revealed improved cable burial, yet the cable remained unburied and suspended in limited areas, which confirms the difficulty of cable burial where the seafloor has boulders, compacted subsurface deposits, and bedrock (Tyco 2006). Under conditions in its sanctuary-issued permit, Pacific Crossing will mitigate risks to fisherman utilizing bottom contact gear through directed outreach concerning cable locations and burial states. The sanctuary has also implemented a monitoring program that has provided important information on the rate of seafloor habitat

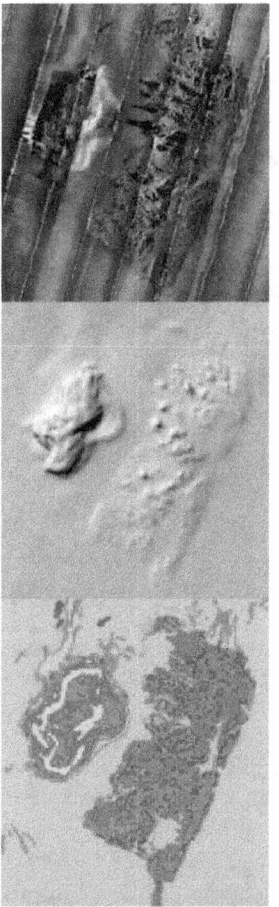

Figure 32. Using texture analysis algorithms, information from side-scan sonar imagery (top plate) and multi-beam bathymetry (middle plate) are combined to create classified habitat images (bottom plate). Image: OCNMS

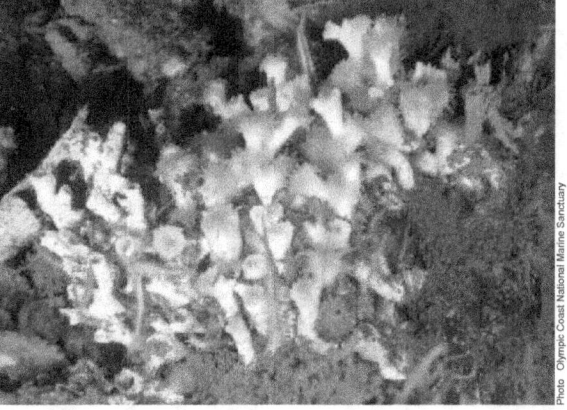

Figure 33. Stony coral *Lophelia pertusa*, characteristic of deepwater coral assemblages in the North Atlantic but less documented in the Pacific, was recently found in the sanctuary at several locations.

Figure 34. Derelict gear is removed from the ocean floor. This net contained numerous dead animals, including seabirds, fish, harbor seals, harbor porpoise and a California sea lion.

recovery following disturbance associated with cable installation, and which will inform future decision-making on similar proposals.

## Living Resources

### *Groundfish Protection/Designation of Essential Fish Habitat*

Recent significant conservation actions applied to the sanctuary area include the establishment of conservation areas to protect groundfish habitat and minimize the bycatch of overfished species. In 2000, the state of Washington prohibited bottom trawling in state waters (Figure 35). More recently, the Pacific Fishery Management Commission and NOAA Fisheries Service designated multiple areas along the West Coast as Essential Fish Habitat (EFH) areas with specific fishing restrictions. Five EFH areas were adopted off the coast of Washington that are closed to non-tribal bottom trawl fishing. One unit, the Olympic 2 EFH Conservation Area closure, is located within the boundary of the sanctuary (Figure 35) and is closed to all types of non-tribal bottom trawl fishing gear, but not all types of bottom-contact gear, such as longline gear. Olympic 2 EFH covers 7 percent of the sanctuary area. The EFH measures also included a prohibition of bottom trawl activity deeper than 700 fathoms West Coast-wide. The EFH areas were implemented through amendment 19 to the Pacific Coast Groundfish Fisheries Management Plan and went into effect in 2006. In addition, Trawl Rockfish Conservation Areas (RCA) are temporary, large-scale closed areas that extend along the entire length of the U.S. West Coast that are expected to be in place until key overfished rockfish species recover, potentially for more than 80 years. Commercial trawl RCA boundaries approximate particular depth contours that can change during the year (Figure 35) and are designed to minimize opportunities for vessels to incidentally take overfished rockfish by eliminating fishing in areas where

and when those overfished species are likely to co-occur with more healthy stocks of groundfish. In 2008, this Trawl RCA covers between 40 and 48 percent of the sanctuary. A Non-trawl RCA (i.e., the RCA for gears other than trawl, such as longline and pot gear for fish) is closed from the shore seaward to 100 fathoms year-round (Figure 35). This Non-trawl RCA applies to 81 percent of the sanctuary. In addition, there are specific area closures within the sanctuary that are permanent in nature and pertain to specific fisheries — the North Coast Commercial Yelloweye RCA that applies to fixed gear (e.g., longlines and pots) and recreational groundfish and halibut fisheries, the North Coast Recreational RCA, and a small Salmon Troll RCA that lies within the North Coast Recreational RCA (Figure 35). It will be important to monitor the EFH and RCAs to detect changes in physical habitat and groundfish populations.

### *Intertidal Habitats*

In response to growing concerns about impacts of increased visitation to the shores, sanctuary and Olympic National Park staff cooperated in an effort to examine the threats and opportunities to protect intertidal resources along the Olympic Coast. Science experts and citizen representatives outlined activities that are potentially degrading to intertidal areas and disturbing to wildlife, and identified a set of ecologically significant habitats and a range of potential management actions, including possible establishment of no-harvest areas, or intertidal reserves. These sites would provide long-term protection of the federally owned shores as human use increases. Intertidal reserves covering roughly 30 percent of the park's shore were incorporated into the park's Final General Management Plan released in March 2008 and will be subject to existing tribal treaty use of such zones.

### *Monitoring Programs*

A variety of monitoring programs have been established in the sanctuary to assess various aspects of population levels, distribution and health of living resources. Seabirds can be considered sentinel species, or indicators of ocean health, because they depend on forage fish and invertebrates for their food. Seabirds, whales and dolphins are monitored during ship-based observations along established transect lines. The sanctuary supports monitoring of pinniped species (seals and sea lions) by state, federal and tribal biologists. The sea otter population size is assessed annually during coordinated aerial and land-based observations in collaboration with the U.S. Geological Survey, U.S. Fish and Wildlife Service, Washington Department of Fish and Wildlife, and the Seattle Aquarium. Olympic Coast sanctuary staff also partner with the University of Washington on the Coastal Observation and Seabird Survey Team (COASST) to monitor seabird mortality on beaches along the Olympic Coast and the Strait of Juan de Fuca. The kelp canopy is monitored annually in collaboration

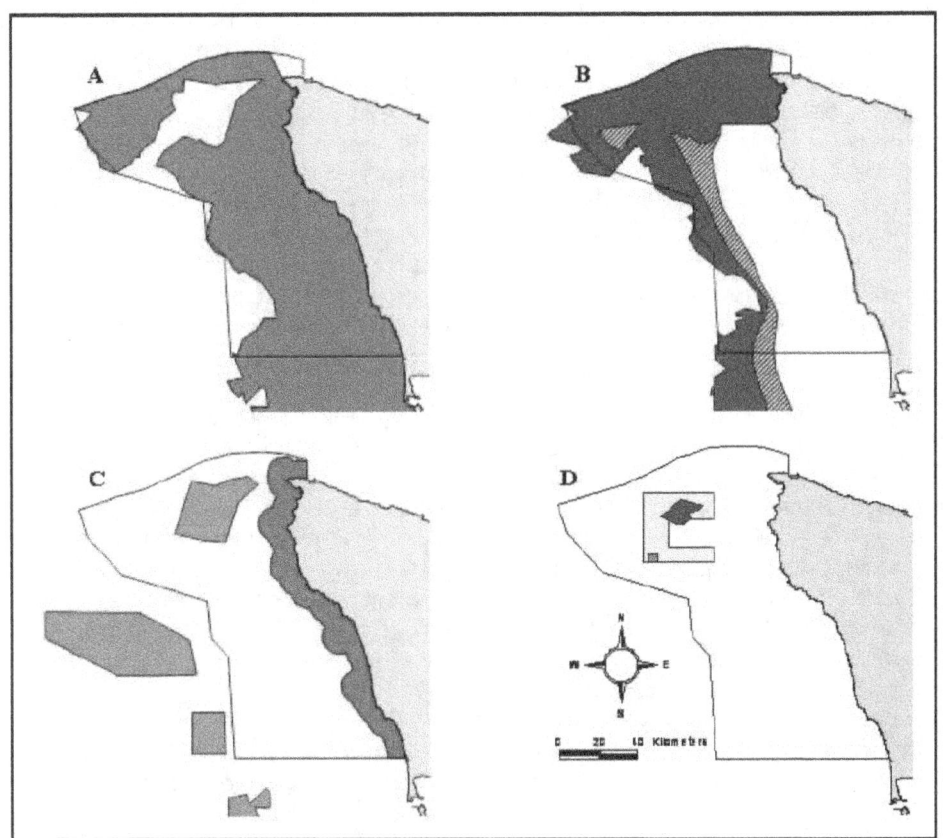

Figure 35. Maps depicting areas offshore from Washington state (gray) and within the Olympic Coast National Marine Sanctuary boundary (black line) subject to fishing closures. (A) Red area is the Non-trawl Rockfish Conservation Area (RCA), which is closed year round to non-tribal commercial longline and fish pot gears. (B) The Trawl RCA is closed to non-tribal commercial trawling with seasonal adjustments to depth contours — solid blue is closed November through February, while both solid and hatch blue approximates areas also closed March through October. (C) Green area is state of Washington waters closed year round to non-tribal commercial trawling, and the orange areas are Essential Fish Habitat conservation areas closed year round to non-tribal commercial trawling. (D) North Coast Yelloweye RCA year-round closures are yellow for recreational groundfish fishing, purple for commercial fixed gear (longline and fish pots) and recreational groundfish, and brown (small box within yellow area) for salmon troll gear. Source: NOAA Fisheries, Northwest Region

with the Washington State Department of Natural Resources. These surveys are conducted with aerial imaging systems to assess total area of kelp coverage. Volunteer organizations also monitor living resources in the sanctuary, such as the Reef Environmental Education Foundation, which conducts visual fish surveys in subtidal habitats.

### Sea Otter Health Study

In 2001 and 2002, the sanctuary joined with the U.S. Fish and Wildlife Service and U.S. Geological Survey to conduct focused re-

search on the health of sea otters off Washington state (Brancato et al. 2006). This study was a response to suspicions that increased disease susceptibility resulting from contaminant-induced immuno-suppression may be responsible for the decline of the California sea otter population, where infectious disease and cardiac disease have been significant mortality factors. With range expansion possible to the south along the Washington coast and east into the Strait of Juan de Fuca, the Washington sea otter population is facing new or additional risks due to increased anthropogenic influences and a different ecosystem. Unlike other marine mammals that migrate extensively, sea otters provide an unusual opportunity to study a mid- to high-trophic level marine consumer inhabiting highly industrial to extremely remote habitats throughout its occurrence in the Northeast Pacific. Because both the sea otters and their principal prey are relatively sedentary, their contaminant burdens should reflect localized contamination. In 2001 and 2002, 32 sea otters were captured, of which 28 were implanted with transmitters to track their movements, and liver and blood samples were collected to evaluate contaminant and pathogen exposure. The results indicate low levels of contaminants in general, but high levels of exposure to morbillivirus and Toxoplasma, the latter of which has been a significant cause of mortality in southern sea otters in California.

### Wildlife Disturbance

To protect seabirds, migratory waterfowl, endangered species, and marine mammals from disturbance and harassment, a sanctuary regulation prohibits flights of motorized aircraft at less than 2,000 feet (610 meters) within 1 nautical mile (1.9 kilometers) of national wildlife refuge islands or the shore, with exceptions for tribal timber operations on reservation lands. To improve familiarity and compliance with this regulation in the recreational pilot community, the sanctuary implemented an outreach program that focused on small aircraft at regional air strips. Sanctuary representatives have attended regional air shows to meet local pilots, talk about the sanctuary's resource protection concerns, and distribute fliers and posters that explain the regulation and its purpose.

### Invasive Species Mitigation and Monitoring

As mentioned above, Washington state has implemented regulations to minimize the risk of invasive species introductions, which require all vessels 300 gross tons or more travelling from foreign ports to exchange of ballast water in the open ocean or to treat the ballast water before discharging in state waters, and to submit ballast water reports. In addition, ships considered U.S. coastal traffic, including Canadian waters, must exchange ballast water no closer than 50 nautical miles (93 kilometers) offshore. The Marine Exchange of Puget Sound reports very high compliance rates with these requirements. Washington Department of Fish and Wildlife and the Washington State Invasive Species Council foster active management to reduce impacts from invasive species.

The sanctuary has sponsored two seasons of rapid assessment (2001 and 2002) of intertidal areas, bringing together a team of taxonomic experts to survey and identify non-indigenous species, as well as to inventory native species. Those surveys documented 10 non-indigenous invertebrate and algal species and, in a joint study with the Smithsonian Environmental Research Center in 2003, two invasive ascidians and one invasive barnacle were also documented (deRivera et al. 2005). A third rapid assessment to cover additional areas of the coastline will be conducted when funding is available. Rigorous monitoring and early detection of non-indigenous species are important tools in minimizing the harmful effects of non-native invaders.

The Olympic National Park and sanctuary staff also conduct long-term intertidal monitoring of both sandy and rocky habitats in order to inventory invertebrates and identify trends in populations. This monitoring program, though not specifically designed to address non-indigenous species, serves as an early warning detection program for non-native species that may become invasive (rapidly reproducing, aggressive or highly competitive with native species) within the region.

The sanctuary also partners with the Washington State Department of Fish and Wildlife and the Makah Tribe in monitoring for the invasive European green crab at sites in Neah Bay and Makah Bay. This non-native crab competes with native species for habitat and food and has proved quite destructive in other areas of the country. To date, no European green crabs have been detected along the sanctuary coast or in Neah Bay, although green crabs have been found just south of the sanctuary boundary in Willapa Bay and also north of the sanctuary along Vancouver Island, B.C.

### Military Activities

The Navy is currently developing two environmental impact assessments for proposed federal actions — one to extend the Quinault Underwater Tracking Range and another to address current, emerging and future fleet training activities in the Northwest Training Range Complex. These multi-year assessments will include opportunities for public input and comment, and are expected to be completed in 2009. Sanctuary staff will be active participants in the environmental assessment process to evaluate potential impacts to sanctuary resources and develop appropriate protection measures. The proposed extension of the Quinault Underwater Tracking Range site could involve the continued testing of non-weaponized equipment in and near the sanctuary.

## Maritime Heritage

Coastal archaeological resources may be negatively impacted by rising sea levels and environmental forces. Under the National Historic Preservation Act, federal agencies are required to inventory and assess resources to determine what, if any, management actions could be taken in an effort to preserve critical sites and material. While programmatic funding has been limited, the sanctuary has participated in individual projects, using small grant funding and staff time as available. Examples of shipwreck studies include Office of National Marine Sanctuaries nationally funded shipwreck surveys of Destruction Island, Quillayute Needles, La Push and Cape Flattery vicinities and intertidal surveys of the wreck Austria conducted with community members and graduate students. Examples involving prehistoric resources include a surface survey of Tatoosh Island, conducted by the Makah Tribal Historic Preservation Officer with sanctuary staff assistance, test pit excavation led by the Makah on paleoshoreline sites on the Makah Reservation (including one excavation funded by a NOAA Maritime Heritage Program minigrant), and periodic visual assessments of known prehistoric sites undertaken cooperatively with the Makah and archaeologists from Olympic National Park. In addition to these activities, sanctuary staff frequently consults with partner organizations as incidents or specific threats arise.

## Climate Change

Changing climatic conditions can not be managed at the level of the sanctuary. However, the sanctuary can assist in documenting the direct effects of climatic changes by recording oceanographic properties such as water temperature and dissolved oxygen levels over time. Using remote moorings, the sanctuary records ocean conditions continuously for the duration of the field season, and — with improved equipment and mooring apparatus — could extend monitoring efforts throughout the year. These data can be shared with other researchers, such as fisheries biologists, to better understand the effects of ocean conditions on these economically important resources. The sanctuary also indirectly assesses responses to climate change in living resources though long-term monitoring of marine birds and mammals, intertidal organisms and invasive species. Associations between ocean conditions, possibly driven by climate change, and the presence of harmful algal blooms or hypoxic conditions are explored through both sanctuary programs and collaborative efforts that include the Olympic Region Harmful Algal Bloom consortium, Ecology and Oceanography of Harmful Algal Blooms, and Partnership for Interdisciplinary Studies of Coastal Oceans.

Coastal archaeological resources may be negatively impacted by rising sea levels. These resources, most on national park and Indian reservation lands, should be inventoried and assessed in order to help managers interpret what, if any, management actions could be taken in an effort to preserve critical sites and material. The sanctuary recognizes this need and will continue to conduct and facilitate these inventories.

# Concluding Remarks

This condition report is the first attempt to describe the relationship between human pressures and the status and trends of natural resources within Olympic Coast National Marine Sanctuary. By doing so, this report helps to identify the pressures and their impacts on marine ecosystems that may warrant monitoring and remediation in the years to come. Overall, the resources protected by the sanctuary appear to be in good to fair condition. Of the 17 resources or questions identified, three appear to be in good condition, six appear to be in good/fair condition, and eight appear to be in fair condition. None of the resources identified was listed in either fair/poor or poor condition.

The Olympic Coast sanctuary has a history of collaborative scientific research among federal, tribal and state agencies, as well as academic and non-government organizations, with studies designed to develop an improved understanding of the ecosystem to inform management and protect the sanctuary's natural resources. In recent years, research conducted in the sanctuary has become focused less on simple characterization and more on oceanographic processes, biogeography, and sources and fates of individual organisms and their contributions to the ecosystem as a whole. It is important to understand the factors that help to structure the resources of the sanctuary, and how uses of its resources may affect their health, viability and longevity. The information presented in this report enables managers to look back and consider past changes in the status of the resources, and provides guidance for continued resource management as future challenges are presented. This is especially important because the sanctuary will soon begin the process of reviewing its management plan, which will enable us to better understand, protect and utilize the nation's marine environment.

## Acknowledgements

*Olympic Coast National Marine Sanctuary would like to acknowledge the assistance of Clancy Environmental Consultants, Inc. who was instrumental in developing the template for this document and providing the initial material under contract to NOAA. We appreciate the efforts of subject area experts who provided responses to questions that guided drafting of the "State of Sanctuary Resources" section of the report:*

*The report benefited significantly from a preliminary review, and we are grateful for comments received on a draft of the report provided by members of the Scientific and Statistical Committee, Habitat Committee, and Groundfish Advisory Panel of the Pacific Fisheries Management Council, NOAA's National Marine Fisheries Service, representatives from the Quileute and Makah Tribes, and the Olympic Coast Sanctuary Advisory Council.*

*Our sincere thanks are also extended to the reviewers of this document: James Delgado, Institute of Nautical Archaeology; Sarah Dzinbal, Washington Department of Natural Resources; Dave Fluharty, University of Washington, School of Marine Affairs; and Rikk Kvitek, California State University, Monterey Bay.*

# Cited Resources

Alter, S.E., E. Rynes, and S.R. Palumbi. 2007. DNA evidence for historic population size and past ecosystem impacts of gray whales. Proceedings of the National Academy of Sciences 104: 15162-15167.

Andrews, A.H, E.E. Cordes, M.M. Mahoney, K. Munk, K.H. Coale, G.M. Cailliet, and J. Heifetz. 2002. Age, growth and radiometric age validation of a deep-sea, habitat-forming gorgonian (Primnoa resedaeformis) from the Gulf of Alaska. Hydrobologia 471: 101-110.

Auster, P.J., R.J. Malatesta, R.W. Langton, L. Watling, P.C. Valentine, C.L.S. Donaldson, E.W. Langton, A.N. Shepard, and I.G. Babb. 1996. The impacts of mobile fishing gear on seafloor habitats in the Gulf of Maine (Northwest Atlantic): implications for conservation of fish populations. Reviews in Fisheries Science 4: 185-202.

Auster, P.J. and R.W. Langton. 1999. The effects of fishing on fish habitat. In: Benaka, L. (ed), pp. 150-187. Fish Habitat: Essential Fish Habitat and Rehabilitation. American Fisheries Society, Bethesda, Maryland.

Babcock E.A., E.K. Pikitch, M.K. McAllister, P. Apostolaki, and C. Santora. 2005. A perspective on the use of spatialized indicators for ecosystem-based fishery management through spatial zoning. ICES Journal of Marine Science for the proceedings of the meeting ICES. Journal of Marine Science. 62: 469-476.

Barth, J.A., B.A. Menge, J. Lubchenco, F. Chan, J.M. Bane, A.R. Kirincich, M.A. McManus, K.J. Nielsen, S.D. Pierce, and L. Washburn. 2007. Delayed upwelling alters nearshore coastal ocean ecosystems in the northern California Current. Proceedings of the National Academy of Sciences 104: 3719-3724.

Berkeley, S.A., C. Chapman, and S.M. Sogard. 2004. Maternal age as a determinant of larval growth and survival in a marine fish, Sebastes melanops. Ecology Letters 85: 1258-1264.

Berry, H.D., T.F. Mumford, and P. Dowty. 2005. Using Historical Data to Estimate Changes in Floating Kelp (Nereocystis luetkeana and Macrosystis integrifolia) in Puget Sound, Washington. In: PSAT (Puget Sound Action Team). 2005. Georgia Basin/Puget Sound Research Conference Proceedings. 2005 Georgia Basin/Puget Sound Research Conference, Seattle, WA, Puget Sound Water Quality Authority.

Blanchette, C.A., M. Miner, P.T. Raimondi, D. Lohse, K.E.K. Heady, and B.R. Broitman. In press. Biogeographical patterns of rocky intertidal communities along the Pacific coast of North America. Journal of Biogeography.

Bowlby, C.E., S.S. Intelmann, G. Galasso, and A. Martin. 2008. Seafloor habitat survey effort in Olympic Coast National Marine Sanctuary. p. 41-43 in Washington State Seafloor Mapping Workshop Proceedings, January 22-23, 2008, Seattle, WA..

Brancato, M. S., J.W. Davis, R. Jameson. C.E. Bowlby, and L. Milonas. 2006. Chemical Contaminants, Pathogen Exposure and General Health Status of Live and Beach-Cast Washington Sea Otters (Enhydra lutris kenyoni). Lacy, WA, Department of Interior, U.S. Fish and Wildlife Service Region 1: 175.

Brancato, M.S., C.E. Bowlby, J. Hyland, S.S. Intelmann, and K. Brenkman. 2007. Observations of Deep Coral and Sponge Assemblages in Olympic Coast National Marine Sanctuary, Washington. Cruise Report: NOAA Ship McArthur II Cruise AR06-06/07. Marine Sanctuaries Conservation Series NMSP-07-03. U.S. Department of Commerce, National Oceanic and Atmospheric Administration, National Marine Sanctuary Program, Silver Spring, MD. 48 pp.

Calambokidis, J., G.H. Steiger, D.K. Ellifrit, B.L. Troutman, and C.E. Bowlby. 2004. Distribution and abundance of humpback whales (Megaptera novaeangliae) and other marine mammals off the northern Washington coast. Fishery Bulletin 102(4): 563-580.

Chan, F., J. A. Barth, J. Lubchenco, A. Kirincich, H. Weeks, W. T. Peterson, and B. A. Menge. 2008. Emergence of anoxia in the California Current large marine ecosystem. Science 319: 920.

Clark, R.C., Jr., J.S. Finley, B.G. Patten, and E.E. deNike. 1975. Long-term chemical and biological effects of a persistent oil spill following the grounding of the General M.C. Meigs. pp. 479-487 Conference on Prevention and Control of Oil Pollution. API/USCG/EPA, San Francisco, CA March 25-27, 1975.

Cockcroft V.G., A.C. Kock, D.A. Lord, and G.J.B. Ross. 1989. Organochlorines in bottlenose dolphins Tursiops truncatus from the east coast of South Africa. South African Journal of Marine Science 8: 207-217.

Collie, J.S., G.A. Escanero, and P.C. Valentine. 1997. Effects of bottom fishing on the benthic megafauna of Georges Bank. Mar. Ecol. Prog. Ser. 155: 159-172.

Dahl, E. J. 2001. Naval Innovation: From Coal to Oil. Joint Forces Quarterly 27: 50-56.

Dayton, P.K., M.J. Tegner, P.E. Parnell, and P.B. Edwards. 1992. Temporal and spatial patterns of disturbance and recovery in a kelp forest community. Ecological Monographs. 62: 421-445.

deRivera, C.E., G.M. Ruiz, J. Crooks, K. Wasson, S. Lonhart, P. Fofonoff, B. Steves, S. Rumrill, M.S. Brancato, S. Pegau, D. Bulthuis, R.K. Preisler, C.G. Schoch, C.E. Bowlby, A. DeVogelaere, M. Crawford, S.R. Gittings, A.H. Hines, L. Takata, K. Larson, T. Huber, A.M. Leyman, E. Collinetti, T. Pascot, S. Shull, M. Anderson, and S. Powell. 2005. Broad-scale non-indigenous species monitoring along the west coast in national marine sanctuaries and national estuarine research reserves. Report to National Fish & Wildlife Foundation. Smithsonian Institute, National Estuarine Research Reserve System, National Marine Sanctuary Program, Washington, D.C. 125 pp.

Dethier, M.N. 1988. A Survey of Intertidal Communities of the Pacific Coastal Area of Olympic National Park, Washington: Final Report. Final Report, National Park Service, Friday Harbor.

Dethier, M.N. 1995. Intertidal monitoring in Olympic National Park, 1995: a turning point. Report to the National Park Service. Friday Harbor Laboratories. Friday Harbor, Washington.

Deuser, W.G. 1975. Reducing environments. In: Riley, J.P. and G. Skirrow (eds). Chemical Oceanography, 2nd ed., vol. 3. Academic Press. pp 1-37.

Devinny, J.S. and L.A. Volse. 1978. Effects of sediments on the development of Macrocystis pyrifera gametophytes. Marine Biology 48: 343-348.

Downs, C.A., G. Shigenaka, J.E. Fauth, C.E. Robinson, and A. Huang. 2002. Cellular physiological assessment of bivalves after chronic exposure to spilled Exxon Valdez crude oil using a novel molecular diagnostic biotechnology. Environmental Science and Technology 36: 2987-2993.

Eldridge, M.B. and B.M. Jarvis. 1995. Temporal and spatial variation in fecundity of yellowtail rockfish. Transactions of the American Fisheries Society 124: 16-25.

EPA (Environmental Protection Agency). 2007. Draft cruise ship assessment report. EPA842-R-07-005. December 2007. Office of Water, Washington, D.C.

Epstein, P.R., T.E. Ford, and R.R. Colwell. 1993. Health and climate change: Marine ecosystems. The Lancet 342:1216-1219.

Erickson, A. 2005. Effects of human trampling in the barnacle zone along a gradient of use in Olympic National Park. Master's Thesis. University of Washington Seattle, WA. 50 pp.

Erickson, A. and J.G. Wullschleger 1998. A preliminary assessment of harvest on the Olympic Coast. Port Angeles, WA, Olympic National Park: 15 pp.

Estes, J.A. and D.O. Duggins 1995. Sea otters and kelp forests in Alaska: generality and variation on a community ecological paradigm" Ecological Monographs 65(1): 75-100.

Estes, J.A., D.O. Duggins, and G.B. Rathbun. 1989. The ecology of extinctions in kelp forest communities Conservation Biology 3(3): 252-264.

Etnoyer, P. and L.E. Morgan 2003. Occurrences of habitat-forming deep sea corals in the northeast Pacific Ocean. Redmond, WA, Marine Conservation Biology Institute: 31.

FERC (Federal Energy Regulatory Commission). 2007. Environmental Assessment for Hydropower License - Makah Bay Offshore Wave Energy Pilot Project. Federal Energy Regulatory Commission. May 2007.

Field, J.C., R.C. Francis, and A. Storm. 2001. Toward a fisheries ecosystem plan for the northern California Current. CalCOFI Report. 42:74-87.

Fluharty, D. 2005. Evolving ecosystem approaches to management of fisheries in the USA. Marine Ecology Progress Series 300:248-253

Foreman, M, W. Callendar, A. MacFadyen, B. Hickey, V. Trainer, A. Pena, R. Thomson, and E. Di Lorenzo. 2007. Juan de Fuca Eddy generation and its relevance to harmful algal bloom development along the outer Washington coast. In: The Changing North Pacific: Previous Patterns, Future Projections and Ecosystem Impacts. North Pacific Marine Science Organization. p. 83.

Fosså, J.H., P.B. Mortensen, and D.M. Furevik. 2002. The deep-water coral Lophelia pertusa in Norwegian waters: distribution and fishery impacts. Hydrobiologia 471: 1-12.

Gaichas, S.K. 2008. A context for ecosystem-based fishery management: Developing concepts of ecosystems and sustainability. Marine Policy 32:393-401.

Galasso, G. 2000. Olympic Coast National Marine Sanctuary Area to be Avoided (ATBA) Education and Monitoring Program. Marine Sanctuaries Conservation Series Marine Sanctuaries Conservation Series MSD-00-1, U.S. Dept. of Commerce, National Oceanic and Atmospheric Administration, Silver Spring, MD. 34 pp.

Grantham, B.A., F. Chan, K.J. Nielsen, D.S. Fox, J.A. Barth, A. Huyer, J. Lubchenco, and B.A. Menge. 2004. Upwelling-driven nearshore hypoxia signals ecosystem and oceanographic changes in the northeast Pacific. Nature 429: 749-754.

Graybill, M.R. and J. Hodder. 1985. Effects of the 1982-83 El Nino on Reproduction of six species of seabirds in Oregon. Pp. 205-210 in: Wooster, W.S. and D.L. Fluharty, Eds., El Niño North. Washington Sea Grant Program, University of Washington, Seattle.

Harvell, C.D., K. Kim, J.M. Burkholder, R.R. Colwell, P.R. Epstein, D.J. Grimes, E.E. Hofmann, E.K. Lipp, A.D. M. E. Osterhaus, R.M. Overstreet, J.W. Porter, G.W. Smith, and G.R. Vasta . 1999. Diseases in the ocean: emerging pathogens, climate links, and anthropogenic factors. Science 285: 1505-1510.

Hass, T. and J.K. Parrish. 2000. Beached Birds: A COASST Field Guide. Second Edition. Wavefall Press, Seattle, WA.

Helton, D. 2003. Wreck removal: a federal perspective. Report 505_Helton_NSC2003, Office of Response and Restoration, NOAA, Seattle, WA. 15 pp.

Heppell, S.S., S.A. Heppell, A.J. Read, and L.B. Crowder. 2005. Effects of fishing on long-lived marine organisms. In E.A. Norse and L.B. Crowder (eds.), pp. 211-231. Marine Conservation Biology: the Science of Maintaining the Sea's Biodiversity, Island Press, Washington. 470 pp.

Hickey, B.M. and N.S. Banas. 2003. Oceanography of the U.S. Pacific Northwest coastal ocean and estuaries with application to coastal ecology. Estuaries 26: 1010-1031.

Hyland, J., C. Cooksey, E. Bowlby, M.S. Brancato, and S. Intelmann. 2005. A pilot survey of deepwater coral/sponge assemblages and their susceptibility to fishing/harvest impacts at the Olympic Coast National Marine Sanctuary (OCNMS). Cruise Report for NOAA Ship McArthur II Cruise AR-04-04: Leg 2. NOAA Technical Memorandum NOS NCCOS 15. NOAA/NOS Center for Coastal Environmental Health and Biomolecular Research, Charleston, SC. 13 p.

Intelmann, S.S. 2006. Habitat mapping effort at the Olympic Coast National Marine Sanctuary – current status and future needs. Marine Sanctuaries Conservation Series. National Oceanic and Atmospheric Administration, National Marine Sanctuary Program, Silver Spring, MD, U.S. Department of Commerce. 29 pp.

Jagielo, T., A. Hoffman, and J. Taggert. 2003. Demersal groundfish densities in trawlable and untrawlable habitats off Washington: implications for the estimation of habitat bias in trawl surveys. Fishery Bulletin 101: 545-565.

Jameson, R.J. and S. Jeffries 2008. Results of the 2007 survey of the reintroduced sea otter population in Washington State. Olympia, WA, Washington Department of Fish and Wildlife: 7p.

Jeffries, S.J., H.R. Huber, J. Calambokidis, and J.L. Laake. 2003. Trends and status of harbor seals in Washington State: 1978-1999. Journal of Wildlife Management 67: 207-218.

Juan de Fuca Eddy Steering Committee. 2004. The Big Eddy - Proceedings of the Western Juan de Fuca Ecosystem Symposium. Western Juan de Fuca Ecosystem Symposium 10-11 May 2004, Institute of Ocean Sciences, Sidney, B.C. Canada. Canadian Parks and Wilderness Society. 141 pp.

Krieger, K. 2001. Coral (Primnoa) impacted by fishing gear in the Gulf of Alaska. In Willison, J.H.M., J. Hall, S.E. Gass, E.L.R. Kenchington, M. Butler, and P. Doherty (eds), pp.106-116. Proceedings of the First International Symposium on Deep-Sea Corals, Halifax, Nova Scotia. 231 pp.

Kvitek, R.G., P.J. Iampietro, and C.E. Bowlby. 1998. Sea otters and benthic prey communities: a direct test of the sea otter as keystone predator in Washington State. Marine Mammal Science 14: 895-902.

Laidre, K., R.J. Jameson, S.J. Jeffries, R.C. Hobbs, C.E. Bowlby, and G.R. VanBlaricom. 2002. Estimates of carrying capacity for sea otters in Washington state. Wildlife Society Bulletin 30: 1172-1181.

Lance, M.M., S.F. Pearson, and M.G. Raphael. 2008. 2007 at-sea Marbled Murrelet population monitoring Research Progress Report WA Department of Fish and Wildlife, Wildlife Science Division, Olympia, WA. 24 pp.

Lance, M.M., S.A. Richardson, and H.L. Allen. 2004. Washington state recovery plan for the sea otter. Washington Department of Fish and Wildlife, Olympia. 91 pp.

Larson, S., R. Jameson, M. Etnier, M. Fleming, and P. Bentzen. 2002. Loss of genetic diversity in sea otters (Enhydra lutris) associated with the fur trade of the 18th and 19th centuries. Molecular Ecology 11:1899-1903.

Linstone, H.A. and M. Turoff. 1975 (ed.). The Delphi Method: Techniques and Applications. available at: http://www.is.njit.edu/pubs/delphi-book.

Long, E.R., D.D. MacDonald, S.L. Smith, and F.D. Calder. 1995. Incidence of adverse biological effects within ranges of chemical concentrations in marine and estuarine sediments. Environmental Management 19(1):81-97.

Lumsden, S.E., T. F. Hourigan, A.W. Bruckner, and G. Dorr. 2007. The state of deep coral ecosystems of the United States. NOAA/National Marine Fisheries Service, Silver Springs, MD. 365 pp.

MacFadyen, A., B.M. Hickey, and M.G.G. Foreman. 2005. Transport of surface waters from the Juan de Fuca eddy region to the Washington coast. Continental Shelf Research 25:2008-2021.

MacFadyen, A., B.M. Hickey, and W.P. Cochlan. 2008. Influences of the Juan de Fuca Eddy on circulation, nutrients, and phytoplankton production in the northern California Current System. Journal of Geophysical Research accepted: 56 pp.

Manuwal, D.A., H.R. Carter, T.S. Zimmerman, and D.L. Orthmeyer, editors. 2001. Biology and Conservation of the Common Murre in California, Oregon, Washington, and British Columbia. Volume 1: Natural history and populations trends. U.S. Geological Survey, Biological Resources Division, Information and Technology Report, Washington, D.C.

Marasco, R.J., Goodman, D., Grimes, C.B., Lawson, P.W., Punt, A.E., Quinn II, T.J. 2007. Ecosystem-based fisheries management: some practical suggestions. Canadian Journal of Fisheries and Aquatic Sciences, 64(6), 928-939.

McCauley, R.D., J. Fewtrell, and A N. Popper. 2003. High intensity anthropogenic sound damages fish ears. Journal of the Acoustic Society of America. 113: 638:642

Miller, M.A., M.E. Grigg, C. Kreuder, E.R. James, A.C. Melli, P.R. Crosbie, D.A. Jessup, J.C. Boothroyd, B.D., and P.A. Conrad. 2004. An unusual genotype of Toxoplasma gondii is common in California sea otters (Enhydra lutris nereis) and is a cause of mortality. International Journal for Parasitology 34:275-284.

Morgan, L.E. and R. Chuenpagdee. 2003. Shifting gears: addressing the collateral impacts of fishing methods in U.S. waters. Washington, DC, Pew Charitable Trust, Marine Conservation Biology Institute: 42.

Morgan, L.E., P. Etnoyer, A.J. Scholz, M. Mertens, and M. Powell. 2005. Conservation and management implication of deep-sea coral and fishing effort distributions in the Northeast Pacific Ocean. In A. Freiwald and J. Roberts (eds), pp. 1171-1187. Cold-water Corals and Ecosystems. Springer-Verlag, Berlin Heidelberg.

Morgan, L.E., F. Tsao, and J.M. Guinotte. 2006. Status of deep sea corals in US waters, with recommendations for their conservation and management. Marine Conservation Biology Institute, Bellevue, WA

Myrberg , A.A. 1990. The effects of man-made noise on the behavior of marine animals. Environment International. 16: 575-586.

National Marine Sanctuary Program. 2004. A monitoring framework for the National Marine Sanctuary System. U.S. Dept. of Commerce, National Oceanic and Atmospheric Administration, National Ocean Service. Silver Spring, MD. 22 pp.

NMFS (National Marine Fisheries Service). 1999. Ecosystem based fisheries management: a report to Congress by the Ecosystem Principles Advisory Panel. Department of Commerce, National Marine Fisheries Service, Silver Springs, MD

NMFS (National Marine Fisheries Service). 2002. Research Plan for West Coast Groundfish. Seattle, WA.

NMFS (National Marine Fisheries Service). 2004. Pacific halibut fisheries; catch sharing plan. Final rule; annual management measures for Pacific halibut fisheries. Federal Register 69(39): 9231-41.

NMFS (National Marine Fisheries Service). 2006. Report on the Status of the U.S. Fisheries for 2006. Report to Congress, NOAA, National Marine Fisheries Service, Washington, D.C.

NOAA (National Oceanic and Atmospheric Administration). 1993. Olympic Coast National Marine Sanctuary Final Environmental Impact Statement/Management Plan Vol. 1. FEIS. Department of Commerce, National Oceanic and Atmospheric Administration, Sanctuaries and Reserves Division, Washington, D.C.

NOAA (National Oceanic and Atmospheric Administration). 2005. Analysis of Remediation Alternatives for the Pacific Crossing-1 North and East Submarine Fiber Optic Cables in the Olympic Coast National Marine Sanctuary. 105 pp.

Norse, E. (ed). 1994. Global marine biological diversity: a strategy for building conservation into decision making. Center for Marine Conservation. Island Press. 383 pp.

NRC (National Research Council). 1999. Sustaining Marine Fisheries. National Research Council, National Academy Press, Washington D.C.

NRC (National Research Council). 2002. Effects of Trawling and Dredging on Seafloor Habitat. Washington, D.C., National Academy Press: 126 pp.

NRC (National Research Council). 2003. Ocean noise and marine mammals. The National Academies Press. Washington, D.C. 204 pp.

NRC (National Research Council). 2006. Dynamic changes in marine ecosystems: fishing, food webs, and future options. Committee on Ecosystem Effects of Fishing: Phase II – Assessment of the Extent of Change and the Implications for Policy. The National Academies Press. Washington, D.C. 154 pp.

NRC, Inc. (Natural Resources Consultants, Inc.). 2008. Rates of marine species mortality caused by derelict fishing nets in Puget Sound, Washington. Prepared for Northwest Straits Initiative. May 15, 2009. 14pp.

Ocean Conservancy. 2007. National Marine Debris Monitoring Program: Final Program Report, Data Analysis and Summary. Submitted to USEPA, Grant No. 83053401-02.

O'Connor, T.P. 2004. The sediment quality guideline, ERL, is not a chemical concentration at the threshold of sediment toxicity. Marine Pollution Bulletin 49(5-6):383-385.

Office of the Governor. 2006. Washington's Ocean Action Plan – Enhancing the Management of Washington State's Ocean and Outer Coast. Volume 1: Final Report of the Washington State Ocean Policy Work Group. Olympia, WA. December 2006.

ONP (Olympic National Park). 2008. Final General Management Plan/Environmental Impact Statement. U.S. Department of the Interior. March 2008.

Pacific Aquaculture Caucus. 2004. State of aquaculture on the west coast: 2004 annual report. PACAQUA, Port Angeles, WA. 25 pp. http://www.pacaqua.org/Documents/StateofAqua4-3.pdf

Paine, R.T. and S.A. Levin. 1981. Intertidal Landscapes: Disturbance and the Dynamics of Pattern. Ecological Monographs, Vol. 51, No. 2, pp. 145-178.

Parrish, J.K., M. Marvier, and R.T. Paine. 2001. Direct and indirect effects: interactions between Bald Eagles and Common Murres. Ecological Applications 11:1858-1869.

Parrish, J.K. and S.G. Zador. 2003. Seabirds as Indicators: An Exploratory Analysis of Physical Forcing in the Pacific Northwest Coastal Environment. Estuaries 26(4): 1044-1057.

Partridge, V. 2007. Condition of coastal waters of Washington State, 2000-2003, a statistical summary. Publication No. 07-03-051, WA State Department of Ecology, Environmental Assessment Program, Olympia, WA.

Pendleton, E.A., E.S. Hammar-Klose, E.R. Thieler, and S.J. Williams. 2004. Coastal Vulnerability Assessment of Olympic National Park to Sea-Level Rise. Open-File Report, Electronic Book 04-1021, U.S. Geological Survey, Woods Hole Science Center, Coastal and Marine Program. 22 pp.

PFMC (Pacific Fishery Management Council). 2005. Amendment 18 (bycatch mitigation program) Amendment 19 (essential fish habitat) to the Pacific coast groundfish fishery management plan for the California, Oregon and Washington groundfish fishery. In: Pacific Fishery Management Council (ed). 98 pp.

PFMC (Pacific Fishery Management Council). 2008a. Status of the Pacific Coast Groundfish Fishery. Stock Assessment and Fishery Evaluation, Volume 1. March 2008. Pacific Fisheries Management Council, Portland, OR.

PFMC (Pacific Fishery Management Council). 2008b. Review of 2007 Ocean Salmon Fisheries. February 2008. Pacific Fisheries Management Council, Portland, OR.

Piatt, J.F., K.J. Kuletz, A.E. Burger, S.A. Hatch, T.P. Birt, M.L. Arimitsu, G.S. Drew, A.M.A. Harding, and K.S. Bixler. 2007. Status Review of the Marbled Murrelet (Brachyramphus marmoratus) in Alaska and British Columbia. Anchorage, AK, U.S. Geological Survey.

Pikitch, E.K., C. Santora, E.A. Babcock, A. Bakun, R. Bonfil, D.O. Conover, P. Dayton, P. Doukakis, D. Fluharty, B. Heneman, E.D. Houde, J. Link, P.A. Livingston, M. Mangel, M.K. McAllister, J. Pope, and K.J. Sainsbury. 2004. Ecosystem-based fishery management. Science 305: 346-347.

PISCO (Partnership for Interdisciplinary Studies of Coastal Oceans). 2002. PISCO Coastal Connections, vol. 1.

PSMFC (Pacific States Marine Fisheries Commission). 2005. Strengthening Scientific Input and Ecosystem-Based Fishery Management for the Pacific and North Pacific Fishery Management Councils. Suggestions from a panel discussion July 19-20, 2005. Seattle, Washington. http://www.fakr.noaa.gov/npfmc/misc_pub/MarascoPaper705.pdf

Ralls, K., J. Ballou, and R.L. Brownell, Jr. 1983. Genetic diversity in California sea otters: Theoretical considerations and management implications. Biological Conservation 25: 209-232.

Raphael, M.G. 2006. Conservation of the Marbled Murrelet under the Northwest Forest Plan. Conservation Biology 20: 297-305.

Raphael, M.G. and T.D. Bloxton. 2008. Breeding ecology of the Marbled Murrelet in Washington State. Project update 2004-2007. Report to U.S.D.A. Forest Service, Pacific Northwest Research Station. Olympia, WA. 32 pp.

Richardson, W.J., C.R. Greene, C.I. Malme, and D.H. Thomson. 1995. Marine mammals and noise. Academic Press. New York, NY. 160 pp.

Rigg, G.B., 1915. The Kelp Beds of Puget Sound, In: Cameron, F.K, Potash from Kelp. United States Department of Agriculture Report #100, Washington D.C., pp. 3-59.

Rogers, A. 2004. The biology, ecology and vulnerability of deep-water coral reefs. Cambridge, International Union for Conservation of Nature & Natural Resources (IUCN): 13 pgs.

Rogers, J.B. and E.K. Pikitch. 1992. Numerical definition of groundfish assemblages caught off the coasts of Oregon and Washington using commercial fishing strategies. Canadian Journal of Fisheries and Aquatic Sciences 49:2648-2656.

Roman, J. and S. R. Palumbi. 2003. Whales before whaling in the North Atlantic. Science 301:508-510.

Ross, P.S. 2006. Fireproof killer whales (Orcinus orca): flame-retardant chemicals and the conservation imperative in the charismatic icon of British Columbia, Canada." Canadian Journal of Fisheries and Aquatic Sciences 63(1): 224-234.

Ross, P.S., G.M. Ellis, M.G. Ikonomou, L.G. Barrett-Lennard, and R.F. Addison. 2000. High PCB concentrations in free-ranging Pacific killer whales, Orcinus orca: Effects of age, sex and dietary preference. Marine Pollution Bulletin 40(6): 504-515.

Scavia, D., J.C. Field, D.F. Boesch, R.W. Buddemeier, V. Burkett, D.R. Cayan, M. Fogarty, M.A. Harwell, R.W. Howarth, C. Mason, D.J. Reed, T.C. Royer, A.H. Sallenger, and J.G. Titus. 2002. Climate change impacts on U.S. Coastal and Marine Ecosystems. Estuaries and Coasts 25: 1559-2723.

Shoji, N.L. 1999. Geospatial analysis of commercial trawl effort within the Olympic Coast National Marine Sanctuary. Nicholas School of the Environment. Master's Thesis. Duke University, Durham, NC. 54pp.

Springer, A.M., J.A. Estes, G.B. van Vlietd, T.M. Williamse, D.F. Doake, E.M. Dannere, K.A. Forney, and B. Pfisterg. 2003. Sequential megafaunal collapse in the North Pacific Ocean: An ongoing legacy of industrial whaling? Pages 12223–12228 Proceedings of the National Academy of Sciences.

Suchanek, T.H. 1979. The Mytilus californianus community: studies on the composition, structure, organization, and dynamics of a mussel bed. PhD thesis, University of Washington.

The Tenyo Maru Oil Spill Natural Resource Trustees. 2000. Final restoration plan and environmental assessment for the Tenyo Maru oil spill. Restoration Plan Cooperating Agencies: Makah Indian Tribe; U.S. Fish and Wildlife Service, Lacy, WA. 70 pp.

Thrush, S.F., P.K. Dayton. 2002. Disturbance to marine benthic habitats by trawling and dredging: implications for marine biodiversity. Annual Review of Ecology and Systematics 33: 449-479.

Trainer, V. 2005. Ecological linkages between physical oceanographic conditions and the seasonal growth and distribution of toxic algal blooms. p. 23-25 in the Proceedings of the Big Eddy - Western Juan de Fuca Ecosystem Symposium, May 10-11, 2004. Sidney, British Columbia.

Trainer, V. and M. Suddleson. 2005. Monitoring approaches for early warning events of domoic acid in Washington state. Oceanography 18: 228-237.

Trites, A.W., V.B. Deecke, E.J. Gregr, J.K.B. Ford, and P.F. Olesiuk. 2007. Killer whales, whaling and sequential megafaunal collapse in the North Pacific: a comparative analysis of the dynamics of marine mammals in Alaska and British Columbia following commercial whaling. Marine Mammal Science 23: 751-765.

Tudela S. and K. Short. 2005. Paradigm shifts, gaps, inertia, and political agendas in ecosystem-based fisheries management. Marine Ecology Progress Series 300:282-286.

Tyco (Tyco Telecommunications). 2006. PC-1 Remediation, Burial Report. March 2007.

USFWS (U.S. Fish and Wildlife Service). 2007. Washington Islands National Wildlife Refuges Comprehensive Conservation Plan and Environmental Assessment. Department of Interior, U.S. Fish and Wildlife Service. 249 pp.

Wade, P.R., V.N. Burkanov, M.E. Dahlheim, N.A. Friday, L.W. Fritz, T.R. Loughlin, S.A. Mizroch, M.M. Muto, D.W. Rice, L.G. Barrett-Lennard, N.A. Black, A.M. Burdin, J. Calambokidis, S. Cerchio, J.K.B. Ford, J.K. Jacobsen, C.O. Matkin, D.R. Matkin, A.V. Mehta, R. Small, J.M. Straley, S.M. McCluskey, and G.R. VanBlaricom. 2007. Killer whales and marine mammal trends in the North Pacific; a re-examination of evidence for sequential megafauna collapse and the prey-switching hypothesis. Marine Mammal Science 23: 766-802.

Wahl, T.R., B. Tweit, and S.G. Mlodinow (eds). 2005. Birds of Washington, Status and Distribution, 1st Ed. edition. Oregon State University Press, Corvallis, OR.

Wahl, T.R. and B. Tweit. 2000. Seabird abundances off Washington, 1972-1998. Western Birds 31:69-88.

Warheit, K.I., and C.W. Thompson. 2003. Common Murre Uria aalge. Pages 12-11 - 21-13 in E.M. Larsen, J.M. Azerrad, and N. Norstrom, editors. Management Recommendations for Washington's Priority Species - Volume IV: Birds. Washington Department of Fish and Wildlife, Olympia, WA.

Washington Department of Fish and Wildlife. 2008. Species of Concern. Olympia WA.

WDOE (Washington State Department of Ecology). 1995. Sediment Management Standards, Chapter 173-204 WAC. Washington State Department of Ecology Publication 96-252. Revised December 1995.

WDOE (Washington State Department of Ecology). 2007. Oil spills in Washington State: a historical analysis. Publication number 97-252. Revised March 2007. Olympia, Washington.

WDOE (Washington State Department of Ecology). 2008. 2007 assessment of cruise ship environmental effects in Washington. Publication number 08-10-032. April 2008. Olympia, Washington.

Washington State Department of Health. 2008. Shellfish growing area annual reports. Website. Retrieved from http://www.doh.wa.gov/ehp/sf/growreports.htm#county Accessed on January 29, 2008.

Watling, L. and E.A. Norse 1999. Clearcutting the ocean floor. Earth Island Journal 14(2): 29-31.

Wessen, G.C. (2003). An assessment and plan for a program of studies addressing prehistoric archaeological sites associated with paleo-shorelines on the Olympic Coast of Washington. Neah Bay, WA. The Makah Cultural and Research Center. 56pp.

Whitney, F.A., Freeland, H.J., and M. Robert. 2006. Decreasing oxygen levels in the interior waters of the subarctic Pacific. Progress in Oceanography 75:179-199.

Whitmire, C.E. and M.E. Clarke. 2007. State of deep sea coral ecosystems in the U.W. Pacific Coast: California to Washington. In: S.E. Lumsden, T.F. Hourigan, A.W. Bruckner and G. Dorr. (eds). The State of Deep Coral Ecosystems in the United States. Silver Spring, MD. NOAA Technical Memorandum CRCP-3: 109-154.

Wilkening, K.E., L.A. Barrie, and M. Engle. 2000. Trans-Pacific Air Pollution. Science 290(5489): 65-67.

Wilson, U.W. 1991. Responses of three seabird species to El Niño events and other warm episodes on the Washington Coast, 1979-1990. The Condor. 93: 853-858.

Worm, B., E.B. Barbier, N.N. Beaumont, J.E. Duffy, C. Folke, B.S. Halpern, J.B. Jackson, H.K. Lotze, F. Micheli, S.R. Palumbi, E. Sala, K.A. Selkoe, J.J. Stachowicz, and R. Watson. 2006. Impacts of Biodiversity Loss on Ocean Ecosystem Services. Science 314: 787-790.

Zabel, R.W., C.J. Harvey, S.L. Katz, T.P. Good, and P.S. Levin. 2003. Ecologically sustainable yield. American Scientist. 91: 150-157.

## Additional Resources

American Park Network, History of Olympic National Park: http://www.americanparknetwork.com/parkinfo/ol/history/

Big Eddy International Marine Ecosystem Initiative: http://www.bigeddy.net/

Channel Islands National Marine Sanctuary, Bridging Our Past Through Shipwrecks: http://channelislands.noaa.gov/shipwreck/shiphome.html

Coastal Observation and Seabird Survey Team: http://www.coasst.org/

Ecology and Oceanography of Harmful Algal Blooms: http://www.ecohabpnw.org/

Intergovernmental Policy Council: http://sanctuaries.noaa.gov/news/features/0107_octribes.html

Makah Cultural and Research Center: http://www.makah.com/mcrchome.htm

Makah Tribe: http://www.makah.com/

Marine Conservation Biology Institute: http://www.mcbi.org/

Marine Protected Areas of the United States: http://www.mpa.gov/

NOAA's Climate Program Office: http://www.climate.noaa.gov/

NOAA's National Center Centers for Coastal Ocean Science: http://coastalscience.noaa.gov/

NOAA's National Marine Fisheries Service: http://www.nmfs.noaa.gov/

NOAA's National Marine Fisheries Service Northwest Regional Office: http://www.nwr.noaa.gov/

NOAA's National Marine Sanctuary Program: http://sanctuaries.noaa.gov/

NOAA's Ocean Explorer: http://www.oceanexplorer.noaa.gov/

NOAA's Office of Ocean Exploration and Research: http://explore.noaa.gov/

NOAA's Office of Response and Restoration: http://response.restoration.noaa.gov/

Northwest Association of Networked Ocean Observing Systems: http://www.nanoos.org/

Northwest Indian Fisheries Commission: http://www.nwifc.wa.gov/

Northwest Straits Commission: http://www.nwstraits.org/

Ocean Futures Society: http://www.oceanfutures.org/

Olympic Coast Alliance: http://www.olympiccoast.org/

Olympic Coast National Marine Sanctuary: http://olympiccoast.noaa.gov/

Olympic National Park: http://www.nps.gov/olym/

Olympic Region Harmful Algal Bloom: http://www.orhab.org/index.html

Oregon State University: Oceanic and Atmospheric Sciences: http://www.coas.oregonstate.edu/

Pacific Fishery Management Council: http://www.pcouncil.org/

Pacific Northwest Seismic Network: http://www.pnsn.org/

Partnership for Interdisciplinary Studies of Coastal Oceans: http://www.piscoweb.org/

Quileute Tribe: http://www.quileutetribe.org/

U.S. Fish & Wildlife Service: Pacific Region: http://www.fws.gov/pacific/

U.S. Geological Survey, Cascades Volcano Observatory: http://vulcan.wr.usgs.gov/

U.S. Geological Survey, Tsunamis and Earthquake Research: http://walrus.wr.usgs.gov/tsunami/

U.S. Geological Survey: http://www.usgs.gov/

Washington Department of Fish and Wildlife: http://wdfw.wa.gov/home.htm

Washington Invasive Species Coalition: http://www.invasivespeciescoalition.org/

Washington Maritime National Wildlife Refuge Complex: http://www.fws.gov/pacific/refuges/field/WA_maritime.htm

Washington Sea Grant Program: http://www.wsg.washington.edu/

Washington State Department of Ecology: http://www.ecy.wa.gov/

Washington State Department of Natural Resources: http://www.dnr.wa.gov/

Washington State Ocean Policy Work Group: http://courses.washington.edu/oceangov/OPWG.html

# Appendix A: Rating Scale for System-Wide Monitoring Questions

The purpose of this appendix is to clarify the 17 questions and possible responses used to report the condition of sanctuary resources in "Condition Reports" for all national marine sanctuaries. Individual staff and partners utilized this guidance, as well as their own informed and detailed understanding of the site to make judgments about the status and trends of sanctuary resources.

The questions derive from the Office of National Marine Sanctuaries' mission, and a system-wide monitoring framework (National Marine Sanctuary Program 2004) developed to ensure the timely flow of data and information to those responsible for managing and protecting resources in the ocean and coastal zone, and to those that use, depend on and study the ecosystems encompassed by the sanctuaries. They are being used to guide staff and partners at each of the 14 sites in the sanctuary system in the development of this first periodic sanctuary condition report. The questions are meant to set the limits of judgments so that responses can be confined to certain reporting categories that will later be compared among all sites and combined. Evaluations of status and trends may be based on interpretation of quantitative and, when necessary, non-quantitative assessments and observations of scientists, managers and users.

Following a brief discussion about each question, statements are presented that were used to judge the status and assign a corresponding color code. These statements are customized for each question. In addition, the following options are available for all questions: "N/A" — the question does not apply; and "Undet." — resource status is undetermined.

Symbols used to indicate trends are the same for all questions: "▲" — conditions appear to be improving; "▯" — conditions do not appear to be changing; "▼" — conditions appear to be declining; and "▢" — trend is undetermined.

## Water Stressors

**1.** Are specific or multiple stressors, including changing oceanographic and atmospheric conditions, affecting water quality and how are they changing?

This is meant to capture shifts in condition arising from certain changing physical processes and anthropogenic inputs. Factors resulting in regionally accelerated rates of change in water temperature, salinity, dissolved oxygen or water clarity could all be judged to reduce water quality. Localized changes in circulation or sedimentation resulting, for example, from coastal construction or dredge spoil disposal, can affect light penetration, salinity regimes, oxygen levels, productivity, waste transport and other factors that influence habitat and living resource quality. Human inputs, generally in the form of contaminants from point or non-point sources, including fertilizers, pesticides, hydrocarbons, heavy metals and sewage, are common causes of environmental degradation, often in combination rather than alone. Certain biotoxins, such as domoic acid, may be of particular interest to specific sanctuaries. When present in the water column, any of these contaminants can affect marine life by direct contact or ingestion, or through bioaccumulation via the food chain.

[Note: Over time, accumulation in sediments can sequester and concentrate contaminants. Their effects may manifest only when the sediments are resuspended during storm or other energetic events. In such cases, reports of status should be made under Question 7 – Habitat contaminants.]

| | | |
|---|---|---|
| ▉ | **Good** | Conditions do not appear to have the potential to negatively affect living resources or habitat quality. |
| ▉ | **Good/Fair** | Selected conditions may preclude full development of living resource assemblages and habitats, but are not likely to cause substantial or persistent declines. |
| ▉ | **Fair** | Selected conditions may inhibit the development of assemblages and may cause measurable but not severe declines in living resources and habitats. |
| ▉ | **Fair/Poor** | Selected conditions have caused or are likely to cause severe declines in some but not all living resources and habitats. |
| ▉ | **Poor** | Selected conditions have caused or are likely to cause severe declines in most if not all living resources and habitats. |

## Water
## Eutrophic
## Condition

**2.** What is the eutrophic condition of sanctuary waters and how is it changing?

Nutrient enrichment often leads to planktonic and/or benthic algae blooms. Some affect benthic communities directly through space competition. Overgrowth and other competitive interactions (e.g., accumulation of algal-sediment mats) often lead to shifts in dominance in the benthic assemblage. Disease incidence and frequency can also be affected by algae competition and the resulting chemistry along competitive boundaries. Blooms can also affect water column conditions, including light penetration and plankton availability, which can alter pelagic food webs. Harmful algal blooms often affect resources, as biotoxins are released into the water and air, and oxygen can be depleted.

| | |
|---|---|
| **Good** | Conditions do not appear to have the potential to negatively affect living resources or habitat quality. |
| **Good/Fair** | Selected conditions may preclude full development of living resource assemblages and habitats, but are not likely to cause substantial or persistent declines. |
| **Fair** | Selected conditions may inhibit the development of assemblages and may cause measurable but not severe declines in living resources and habitats. |
| **Fair/Poor** | Selected conditions have caused or are likely to cause severe declines in some but not all living resources and habitats. |
| **Poor** | Selected conditions have caused or are likely to cause severe declines in most if not all living resources and habitats. |

## Water
## Human Health

**3.** Do sanctuary waters pose risks to human health and how are they changing?

Human health concerns are generally aroused by evidence of contamination (usually bacterial or chemical) in bathing waters or fish intended for consumption. They also emerge when harmful algal blooms are reported or when cases of respiratory distress or other disorders attributable to harmful algal blooms increase dramatically. Any of these conditions should be considered in the course of judging the risk to humans posed by waters in a marine sanctuary.

Some sites may have access to specific information on beach and shellfish conditions. In particular, beaches may be closed when criteria for safe water body contact are exceeded, or shellfish harvesting may be prohibited when contaminant loads or infection rates exceed certain levels. These conditions can be evaluated in the context of the descriptions below.

| | |
|---|---|
| **Good** | Conditions do not appear to have the potential to negatively affect human health. |
| **Good/Fair** | Selected conditions that have the potential to affect human health may exist but human impacts have not been reported. |
| **Fair** | Selected conditions have resulted in isolated human impacts, but evidence does not justify widespread or persistent concern. |
| **Fair/Poor** | Selected conditions have caused or are likely to cause severe impacts, but cases to date have not suggested a pervasive problem. |
| **Poor** | Selected conditions warrant widespread concern and action, as large-scale, persistent and/or repeated severe impacts are likely or have occurred. |

## Water
## Human Activities

**4.** **What are the levels of human activities that may influence water quality and how are they changing?**

Among the human activities in or near sanctuaries that affect water quality are those involving direct discharges (transiting vessels, visiting vessels, onshore and offshore industrial facilities, public wastewater facilities), those that contribute contaminants to stream, river, and water control discharges (agriculture, runoff from impermeable surfaces through storm drains, conversion of land use), and those releasing airborne chemicals that subsequently deposit via particulates at sea (vessels, land-based traffic, power plants, manufacturing facilities, refineries). In addition, dredging and trawling can cause resuspension of contaminants in sediments.

**Good**     Few or no activities occur that are likely to negatively affect water quality.

**Good/Fair**     Some potentially harmful activities exist, but they do not appear to have had a negative effect on water quality.

**Fair**     Selected activities have resulted in measurable resource impacts, but evidence suggests effects are localized, not widespread.

**Fair/Poor**     Selected activities have caused or are likely to cause severe impacts, and cases to date suggest a pervasive problem.

**Poor**     Selected activities warrant widespread concern and action, as large-scale, persistent and/or repeated severe impacts have occurred or are likely to occur.

## Habitat
## Abundance &
## Distribution

**5.** **What are the abundance and distribution of major habitat types and how are they changing?**

Habitat loss is of paramount concern when it comes to protecting marine and terrestrial ecosystems. Of greatest concern to sanctuaries are changes caused, either directly or indirectly, by human activities. The loss of shoreline is recognized as a problem indirectly caused by human activities. Habitats with submerged aquatic vegetation are often altered by changes in water conditions in estuaries, bays, and nearshore waters. Intertidal zones can be affected for long periods by spills or by chronic pollutant exposure. Beaches and haul-out areas can be littered with dangerous marine debris, as can the water column or benthic habitats. Sandy subtidal areas and hardbottoms are frequently disturbed or destroyed by trawling. Even rocky areas several hundred meters deep are increasingly affected by certain types of trawls, bottom longlines and fish traps. Groundings, anchors and divers damage submerged reefs. Cables and pipelines disturb corridors across numerous habitat types and can be destructive if they become mobile. Shellfish dredging removes, alters and fragments habitats.

The result of these activities is the gradual reduction of the extent and quality of marine habitats. Losses can often be quantified through visual surveys and to some extent using high-resolution mapping. This question asks about the quality of habitats compared to those that would be expected without human impacts. The status depends on comparison to a baseline that existed in the past - one toward which restoration efforts might aim.

**Good**     Habitats are in pristine or near-pristine condition and are unlikely to preclude full community development.

**Good/Fair**     Selected habitat loss or alteration has taken place, precluding full development of living resource assemblages, but it is unlikely to cause substantial or persistent degradation in living resources or water quality.

**Fair**     Selected habitat loss or alteration may inhibit the development of assemblages, and may cause measurable but not severe declines in living resources or water quality.

**Fair/Poor**     Selected habitat loss or alteration has caused or is likely to cause severe declines in some but not all living resources or water quality.

**Poor**     Selected habitat loss or alteration has caused or is likely to cause severe declines in most if not all living resources or water quality.

## Habitat Structure

**6.** | **What is the condition of biologically structured habitats and how is it changing?**

Many organisms depend on the integrity of their habitats and that integrity is largely determined by the condition of particular living organisms. Coral reefs may be the best known examples of such biologically-structured habitats. Not only is the substrate itself biogenic, but the diverse assemblages residing within and on the reefs depend on and interact with each other in tightly linked food webs. They also depend on each other for the recycling of wastes, hygiene and the maintenance of water quality, among other requirements.

Kelp beds may not be biogenic habitats to the extent of coral reefs, but kelp provides essential habitat for assemblages that would not reside or function together without it. There are other communities of organisms that are also similarly co-dependent, such as hard-bottom communities, which may be structured by bivalves, octocorals, coralline algae or other groups that generate essential habitat for other species. Intertidal assemblages structured by mussels, barnacles and algae are another example, seagrass beds another. This question is intended to address these types of places where organisms form structures (habitats) on which other organisms depend.

**Good**     Habitats are in pristine or near-pristine condition and are unlikely to preclude full community development.

**Good/Fair**     Selected habitat loss or alteration has taken place, precluding full development of living resources, but it is unlikely to cause substantial or persistent degradation in living resources or water quality.

**Fair**     Selected habitat loss or alteration may inhibit the development of living resources and may cause measurable but not severe declines in living resources or water quality.

**Fair/Poor**     Selected habitat loss or alteration has caused or is likely to cause severe declines in some but not all living resources or water quality.

**Poor**     Selected habitat loss or alteration has caused or is likely to cause severe declines in most if not all living resources or water quality.

## Habitat Contaminants

**7.** | **What are the contaminant concentrations in sanctuary habitats and how are they changing?**

This question addresses the need to understand the risk posed by contaminants within benthic formations, such as soft sediments, hard bottoms, or biogenic organisms. In the first two cases, the contaminants can become available when released via disturbance. They can also pass upwards through the food chain after being ingested by bottom dwelling prey species. The contaminants of concern generally include pesticides, hydrocarbons and heavy metals, but the specific concerns of individual sanctuaries may differ substantially.

**Good**     Contaminants do not appear to have the potential to negatively affect living resources or water quality.

**Good/Fair**     Selected contaminants may preclude full development of living resource assemblages, but are not likely to cause substantial or persistent degradation.

**Fair**     Selected contaminants may inhibit the development of assemblages and may cause measurable but not severe declines in living resources or water quality.

**Fair/Poor**     Selected contaminants have caused or are likely to cause severe declines in some but not all living resources or water quality.

**Poor**     Selected contaminants have caused or are likely to cause severe declines in most if not all living resources or water quality.

## Habitat
## Human Activities

**8.** | **What are the levels of human activities that may influence habitat quality and how are they changing?**

Human activities that degrade habitat quality do so by affecting structural (geological), biological, oceanographic, acoustic or chemical characteristics. Structural impacts include removal or mechanical alteration, including various fishing techniques (trawls, traps, dredges, longlines and even hook-and-line in some habitats), dredging channels and harbors and dumping spoil, vessel groundings, anchoring, laying pipelines and cables, installing offshore structures, discharging drill cuttings, dragging tow cables, and placing artificial reefs. Removal or alteration of critical biological components of habitats can occur along with several of the above activities, most notably trawling, groundings and cable drags. Marine debris, particularly in large quantities (e.g., lost gill nets and other types of fishing gear), can affect both biological and structural habitat components. Changes in water circulation often occur when channels are dredged, fill is added, coastal areas are reinforced, or other construction takes place. These activities affect habitat by changing food delivery, waste removal, water quality (e.g., salinity, clarity and sedimentation), recruitment patterns and a host of other factors. Acoustic impacts can occur to water column habitats and organisms from acute and chronic sources of anthropogenic noise (e.g., shipping, boating, construction). Chemical alterations most commonly occur following spills and can have both acute and chronic impacts.

| | |
|---|---|
| **Good** | Few or no activities occur that are likely to negatively affect habitat quality. |
| **Good/Fair** | Some potentially harmful activities exist, but they do not appear to have had a negative effect on habitat quality. |
| **Fair** | Selected activities have resulted in measurable habitat impacts, but evidence suggests effects are localized, not widespread. |
| **Fair/Poor** | Selected activities have caused or are likely to cause severe impacts, and cases to date suggest a pervasive problem. |
| **Poor** | Selected activities warrant widespread concern and action, as large-scale, persistent and/or repeated severe impacts have occurred or are likely to occur. |

## Living Resources
## Biodiversity

**9.** | **What is the status of biodiversity and how is it changing?**

This is intended to elicit thought and assessment of the condition of living resources based on expected biodiversity levels and the interactions between species. Intact ecosystems require that all parts not only exist, but that they function together, resulting in natural symbioses, competition and predator-prey relationships. Community integrity, resistance and resilience all depend on these relationships. Abundance, relative abundance, trophic structure, richness, H' diversity, evenness and other measures are often used to assess these attributes.

| | |
|---|---|
| **Good** | Biodiversity appears to reflect pristine or near-pristine conditions and promotes ecosystem integrity (full community development and function). |
| **Good/Fair** | Selected biodiversity loss has taken place, precluding full community development and function, but it is unlikely to cause substantial or persistent degradation of ecosystem integrity. |
| **Fair** | Selected biodiversity loss may inhibit full community development and function and may cause measurable but not severe degradation of ecosystem integrity. |
| **Fair/Poor** | Selected biodiversity loss has caused or is likely to cause severe declines in some but not all ecosystem components and reduce ecosystem integrity. |
| **Poor** | Selected biodiversity loss has caused or is likely to cause severe declines in ecosystem integrity. |

## Living Resources
### Extracted Species

**10.** | **What is the status of environmentally sustainable fishing and how is it changing?**

Commercial and recreational harvesting are highly selective activities, for which fishers and collectors target a limited number of species, and often remove high proportions of populations. In addition to removing significant amounts of biomass from the ecosystem, reducing its availability to other consumers, these activities tend to disrupt specific and often critical food web links. When too much extraction occurs (i.e. ecologically unsustainable harvesting), trophic cascades ensue, resulting in changes in the abundance of non-targeted species as well. It also reduces the ability of the targeted species to replenish populations at a rate that supports continued ecosystem integrity.

It is essential to understand whether removals are occurring at ecologically sustainable levels. Knowing extraction levels and determining the impacts of removal are both ways that help gain this understanding. Measures for target species of abundance, catch amounts or rates (e.g., catch per unit effort), trophic structure and changes in non-target species abundance are all generally used to assess these conditions.

Other issues related to this question include whether fishers are using gear that is compatible with the habitats being fished and whether that gear minimizes by-catch and incidental take of marine mammals. For example, bottom-tending gear often destroys or alters both benthic structure and non-targeted animal and plant communities. "Ghost fishing" occurs when lost traps continue to capture organisms. Lost or active nets, as well as lines used to mark and tend traps and other fishing gear, can entangle marine mammals. Any of these could be considered indications of environmentally unsustainable fishing techniques.

| | |
|---|---|
| **Good** | Extraction does not appear to affect ecosystem integrity (full community development and function). |
| **Good/Fair** | Extraction takes place, precluding full community development and function, but it is unlikely to cause substantial or persistent degradation of ecosystem integrity. |
| **Fair** | Extraction may inhibit full community development and function and may cause measurable but not severe degradation of ecosystem integrity. |
| **Fair/Poor** | Extraction has caused or is likely to cause severe declines in some but not all ecosystem components and reduce ecosystem integrity. |
| **Poor** | Extraction has caused or is likely to cause severe declines in ecosystem integrity. |

## Living Resources
### Non-Indigenous Species

**11.** | **What is the status of non-indigenous species and how is it changing?**

Non-indigenous species are generally considered problematic and candidates for rapid response, if found soon after invasion. For those that become established, their impacts can sometimes be assessed by quantifying changes in the affected native species. This question allows sanctuaries to report on the threat posed by non-indigenous species. In some cases, the presence of a species alone constitutes a significant threat (certain invasive algae). In other cases, impacts have been measured and may or may not significantly affect ecosystem integrity.

| | |
|---|---|
| **Good** | Non-indigenous species are not suspected or do not appear to affect ecosystem integrity (full community development and function). |
| **Good/Fair** | Non-indigenous species exist, precluding full community development and function, but are unlikely to cause substantial or persistent degradation of ecosystem integrity. |
| **Fair** | Non-indigenous species may inhibit full community development and function and may cause measurable but not severe degradation of ecosystem integrity. |
| **Fair/Poor** | Non-indigenous species have caused or are likely to cause severe declines in some but not all ecosystem components and reduce ecosystem integrity. |
| **Poor** | Non-indigenous species have caused or are likely to cause severe declines in ecosystem integrity. |

## Living Resources
## Key Species

**12.** | **What is the status of key species and how is it changing?**

Certain species can be defined as "key" within a marine sanctuary. Some might be keystone species, that is, species on which the persistence of a large number of other species in the ecosystem depends - the pillar of community stability. Their functional contribution to ecosystem function is disproportionate to their numerical abundance or biomass and their impact is therefore important at the community or ecosystem level. Their removal initiates changes in ecosystem structure and sometimes the disappearance of or dramatic increase in the abundance of dependent species. Keystone species may include certain habitat modifiers, predators, herbivores and those involved in critical symbiotic relationships (e.g. cleaning or co-habitating species).

Other key species may include those that are indicators of ecosystem condition or change (e.g., particularly sensitive species), those targeted for special protection efforts, or charismatic species that are identified with certain areas or ecosystems. These may or may not meet the definition of keystone, but do require assessments of status and trends.

| | |
|---|---|
| **Good** | Key and keystone species appear to reflect pristine or near-pristine conditions and may promote ecosystem integrity (full community development and function). |
| **Good/Fair** | Selected key or keystone species are at reduced levels, perhaps precluding full community development and function, but substantial or persistent declines are not expected. |
| **Fair** | The reduced abundance of selected keystone species may inhibit full community development and function and may cause measurable but not severe degradation of ecosystem integrity; or selected key species are at reduced levels, but recovery is possible. |
| **Fair/Poor** | The reduced abundance of selected keystone species has caused or is likely to cause severe declines in some but not all ecosystem components, and reduce ecosystem integrity; or selected key species are at substantially reduced levels, and prospects for recovery are uncertain. |
| **Poor** | The reduced abundance of selected keystone species has caused or is likely to cause severe declines in ecosystem integrity; or selected key species are at severely reduced levels, and recovery is unlikely. |

## Living Resources
## Health of Key Species

**13.** | **What is the condition or health of key species and how is it changing?**

For those species considered essential to ecosystem integrity, measures of their condition can be important to determining the likelihood that they will persist and continue to provide vital ecosystem functions. Measures of condition may include growth rates, fecundity, recruitment, age-specific survival, tissue contaminant levels, pathologies (disease incidence tumors, deformities), the presence and abundance of critical symbionts, or parasite loads. Similar measures of condition may also be appropriate for other key species (indicator, protected or charismatic species). In contrast to the question about keystone species (#12 above), the impact of changes in the abundance or condition of key species is more likely to be observed at the population or individual level and less likely to result in ecosystem or community effects.

| | |
|---|---|
| **Good** | The condition of key resources appears to reflect pristine or near-pristine conditions. |
| **Good/Fair** | The condition of selected key resources is not optimal, perhaps precluding full ecological function, but substantial or persistent declines are not expected. |
| **Fair** | The diminished condition of selected key resources may cause a measurable but not severe reduction in ecological function, but recovery is possible. |
| **Fair/Poor** | The comparatively poor condition of selected key resources makes prospects for recovery uncertain. |
| **Poor** | The poor condition of selected key resources makes recovery unlikely. |

## Living Resources
## Human Activities

**14.** | **What are the levels of human activities that may influence living resource quality and how are they changing?**

Human activities that degrade living resource quality do so by causing a loss or reduction of one or more species, by disrupting critical life stages, by impairing various physiological processes, or by promoting the introduction of non-indigenous species or pathogens. (Note: Activities that impact habitat and water quality may also affect living resources. These activities are dealt with in Questions 4 and 8, and many are repeated here as they also have direct effect on living resources).

Fishing and collecting are the primary means of removing resources. Bottom trawling, seine-fishing and the collection of ornamental species for the aquarium trade are all common examples, some being more selective than others. Chronic mortality can be caused by marine debris derived from commercial or recreational vessel traffic, lost fishing gear and excess visitation, resulting in the gradual loss of some species.

Critical life stages can be affected in various ways. Mortality to adult stages is often caused by trawling and other fishing techniques, cable drags, dumping spoil or drill cuttings, vessel groundings or persistent anchoring. Contamination of areas by acute or chronic spills, discharges by vessels, or municipal and industrial facilities can make them unsuitable for recruitment; the same activities can make nursery habitats unsuitable. Although coastal armoring and construction can increase the availability of surfaces suitable for the recruitment and growth of hard bottom species, the activity may disrupt recruitment patterns for other species (e.g., intertidal soft bottom animals) and habitat may be lost.

Spills, discharges, and contaminants released from sediments (e.g., by dredging and dumping) can all cause physiological impairment and tissue contamination. Such activities can affect all life stages by reducing fecundity, increasing larval, juvenile, and adult mortality, reducing disease resistance, and increasing susceptibility to predation. Bioaccumulation allows some contaminants to move upward through the food chain, disproportionately affecting certain species.

Activities that promote introductions include bilge discharges and ballast water exchange, commercial shipping and vessel transportation. Releases of aquarium fish can also lead to species introductions.

| | | |
|---|---|---|
| ▮ | **Good** | Few or no activities occur that are likely to negatively affect living resource quality. |
| ▮ | **Good/Fair** | Some potentially harmful activities exist, but they do not appear to have had a negative effect on living resource quality. |
| ▮ | **Fair** | Selected activities have resulted in measurable living resource impacts, but evidence suggests effects are localized, not widespread. |
| ▮ | **Fair/Poor** | Selected activities have caused or are likely to cause severe impacts, and cases to date suggest a pervasive problem. |
| ▮ | **Poor** | Selected activities warrant widespread concern and action, as large-scale, persistent and/or repeated severe impacts have occurred or are likely to occur. |

## Maritime Archaeological Resources
### Integrity

**15.** | **What is the integrity of known maritime archaeological resources and how is it changing?**

The condition of archaeological resources in a marine sanctuary significantly affects their value for science and education, as well as the resource's eligibility for listing in the National Register of Historic Places. Assessments of archaeological sites include evaluation of the apparent levels of site integrity, which are based on levels of previous human disturbance and the level of natural deterioration. The historical, scientific and educational values of sites are also evaluated and are substantially determined and affected by site condition.

**Good**    Known archaeological resources appear to reflect little or no unexpected disturbance.

**Good/Fair**    Selected archaeological resources exhibit indications of disturbance, but there appears to have been little or no reduction in historical, scientific or educational value.

**Fair**    The diminished condition of selected archaeological resources has reduced, to some extent, their historical, scientific or educational value, and may affect the eligibility of some sites for listing in the National Register of Historic Places.

**Fair/Poor**    The diminished condition of selected archaeological resources has substantially reduced their historical, scientific or educational value, and is likely to affect their eligibility for listing in the National Register of Historic Places.

**Poor**    The degraded condition of known archaeological resources in general makes them ineffective in terms of historical, scientific or educational value, and precludes their listing in the National Register of Historic Places.

## Maritime Archaeological Resources
### Threat to Environment

**16.** | **Do known maritime archaeological resources pose an environmental hazard and how is this threat changing?**

The sinking of a ship potentially introduces hazardous materials into the marine environment. This danger is true for historic shipwrecks as well. The issue is complicated by the fact that shipwrecks older than 50 years may be considered historical resources and must, by federal mandate, be protected. Many historic shipwrecks, particularly early to mid-20th century, still have the potential to retain oil and fuel in tanks and bunkers. As shipwrecks age and deteriorate, the potential for release of these materials into the environment increases.

**Good**    Known maritime archaeological resources pose few or no environmental threats.

**Good/Fair**    Selected maritime archaeological resources may pose isolated or limited environmental threats, but substantial or persistent impacts are not expected.

**Fair**    Selected maritime archaeological resources may cause measurable, but not severe, impacts to certain sanctuary resources or areas, but recovery is possible.

**Fair/Poor**    Selected maritime archaeological resources pose substantial threats to certain sanctuary resources or areas, and prospects for recovery are uncertain.

**Poor**    Selected maritime archaeological resources pose serious threats to sanctuary resources, and recovery is unlikely.

## Maritime Archaeological Resources
## Human Activities

**17.** What are the levels of human activities that may influence maritime archaeological resource quality and how are they changing?

Some human maritime activities threaten the physical integrity of submerged archaeological resources. Archaeological site integrity is compromised when elements are moved, removed or otherwise damaged. Threats come from looting by divers, inadvertent damage by scuba diving visitors, improperly conducted archaeology that does not fully document site disturbance, anchoring, groundings, and commercial and recreational fishing activities, among others.

| | |
|---|---|
| **Good** | Few or no activities occur that are likely to negatively affect maritime archaeological resource integrity. |
| **Good/Fair** | Some potentially relevant activities exist, but they do not appear to have had a negative effect on maritime archaeological resource integrity. |
| **Fair** | Selected activities have resulted in measurable impacts to maritime archaeological resources, but evidence suggests effects are localized, not widespread. |
| **Fair/Poor** | Selected activities have caused or are likely to cause severe impacts, and cases to date suggest a pervasive problem. |
| **Poor** | Selected activities warrant widespread concern and action, as large-scale, persistent, and/or repeated severe impacts have occurred or are likely to occur. |

# Appendix B:  Consultation with Experts and Document Review

The process for preparing condition reports involves a combination of accepted techniques for collecting and interpreting information gathered from subject matter experts. The approach varies somewhat from sanctuary to sanctuary, in order to accommodate differing styles for working with partners. The Olympic Coast National Marine Sanctuary approach was closely related to the Delphi Method, a technique designed to organize group communication among a panel of geographically dispersed experts by using questionnaires, ultimately facilitating the formation of a group judgment (Linstone and Turoff 1975). This method can be applied when it is necessary for decision-makers to combine the testimony of a group of experts, whether in the form of facts or informed opinion, or both, into a single useful statement.

The Delphi Method relies on repeated interactions with experts who respond to questions with a limited number of choices to arrive at the best supported answers. Feedback to the experts allows them to refine their views, gradually moving the group toward the most agreeable judgment. For condition reports, the Office of National Marine Sanctuaries uses 17 questions related to the status and trends of sanctuary resources, with accompanying descriptions and five possible choices that describe resource condition.

In order to address the 17 questions, sanctuary staff selected and consulted outside experts familiar with water quality, living resources, habitat, and maritime archaeological resources. Some experts were recommended by key partners, including the Intergovernmental Policy Council (IPC), the University of Washington, the Washington Dept. of Fish and Wildlife, and the U.S. Geological Survey. Experts represented various affiliations including the Washington State Departments of Archaeology and Historic Preservation, Ecology, Fish and Wildlife, and Natural Resources; Quinault Indian Nation; Hoh Tribe; Quileute Tribe; Makah Tribe; Coastal Maritime Archaeology Resources; Natural Resource Consultants Inc.; Wessen & Associates Inc.; NOAA (Fisheries and Office of National Marine Sanctuaries); Northwest Indian Fisheries Commission; Olympic National Park; University of Chicago Department of Ecology and Evolution; U.S. Fish and Wildlife Service; and University of Washington (School of Oceanography and Applied Physics Laboratory).

Expert opinion was solicited electronically and through one-on-one contact via phone calls and/or e-mails. Background material was provided to the experts in order to develop a consistent understanding of the project and the questions. Experts were asked to utilize Appendix A, which accompanies every Sanctuary's report, to guide their responses. Appendix A clarifies the set of questions and presents standardized statements that are used to describe the status and assign a corresponding color code on a scale from "good" to "poor." These statements are customized for each question.

During the initial request for response to questions, a total of 80 experts were contacted and 28 responded. They were asked to rate resource status and trends, based on guidance provided, and submit supplemental comments, data, graphics, literature citations, Web site links and other relevant information.

The combined input of all experts was considered by a writing team composed of individuals from the sanctuary and the national office. They tallied and discussed ratings and accompanying com-

ments, and summarized the input in a written draft that included a proposed status rating and a proposed trend for each question. The initial ratings represented agreement by the writing team, based on interpretation of quantitative and, when necessary, non-quantitative expert input, as well as other available information, such as assessments and observations of scientists, managers and users. In some cases, certain input was not used because it was either not relevant to the question it accompanied, or too narrowly focused to address the question. Nevertheless, the ratings and text are intended to summarize the opinions and uncertainty expressed by experts, who based their input on knowledge and perceptions of local conditions. Comments and citations received from the experts were included, as appropriate, in text supporting the ratings.

This draft document was sent back to the subject experts for what was called an "initial review," a 21-day period that allows them to ensure that the report accurately reflected their input, identify information gaps, provide comments or suggest revisions to the ratings and text. Upon receiving those comments, the writing team revised the text and ratings as they deemed appropriate. The final interpretation, ratings and text in the draft condition report were the responsibility of sanctuary staff, with final approval by the sanctuary superintendent. To emphasize this important point, authorship of the report is attributed to the sanctuary alone. Subject experts were not authors, though their efforts and affiliations are acknowledged in the report.

The second phase of review, called invited review, involved particularly important partners in research and resource management, including state natural resource managers, regional fisheries science centers, NOAA's National Marine Fisheries Service, and the Pacific Fisheries Management Council advisory committees (Scientific and Statistical Committee, Habitat Committee, and Groundfish Advisory Panel). Review was also requested from stakeholder representatives on the Olympic Coast Sanctuary Advisory Council and from the sanctuary system's West Coast Regional Office. These bodies were asked to review the technical merits of resource ratings and accompanying text, as well as to point out any omissions or factual errors. The comments and recommendations of invited reviewers were received, considered by sanctuary staff and incorporated, as appropriate, into a final draft document.

A draft final report was then sent to James Delgado, Institute of Nautical Archaeology; Sarah Dzinbal, Washington Department of Natural Resources; Dave Fluharty, University of Washington, School of Marine Affairs; and Rikk Kvitek, California State University, Monterey Bay, who served as external peer reviewers. This external peer review is a requirement that started in December 2004, when the White House Office of Management and Budget (OMB) issued a Final Information Quality Bulletin for Peer Review (OMB bulletin) establishing peer review standards that would enhance the quality and credibility of the federal government's scientific information. Along with other information, these standards apply to Influential Scientific Information, which is information that can reasonably be determined to have a "clear and substantial impact on important public policies or private sector decisions." The condition reports are considered Influential Scientific Information. For this reason, these reports are subject to the review requirements of both the Information Quality Act and the OMB bulletin guidelines. Therefore, following the completion of every condition report, they are reviewed by a minimum of three individuals who are considered to be experts in their field, were not involved in the development of the report, and are not Office of National Marine Sanctuaries employees. Comments from these peer reviews were incorporated into the final text of the report. Furthermore, OMB bulletin guidelines require that reviewer comments, names and affiliations be posted on the agency's Web site: http://www.osec.doc.gov/cio/oipr/pr_plans.htm. Reviewer comments, however, are not attributed to specific individuals. Reviewer comments are posted at the same time as with the formatted final document.

## Notes